SEAT *of* POWER

SEAT *of* POWER

TULSA'S ARDUOUS PURSUIT *of* GOVERNANCE
& THE HOUSE STRONG ENOUGH TO HOLD IT

DOUGLAS MILLER

JOHN HAMILL

müllerhaus
[LEGACY]

TULSA

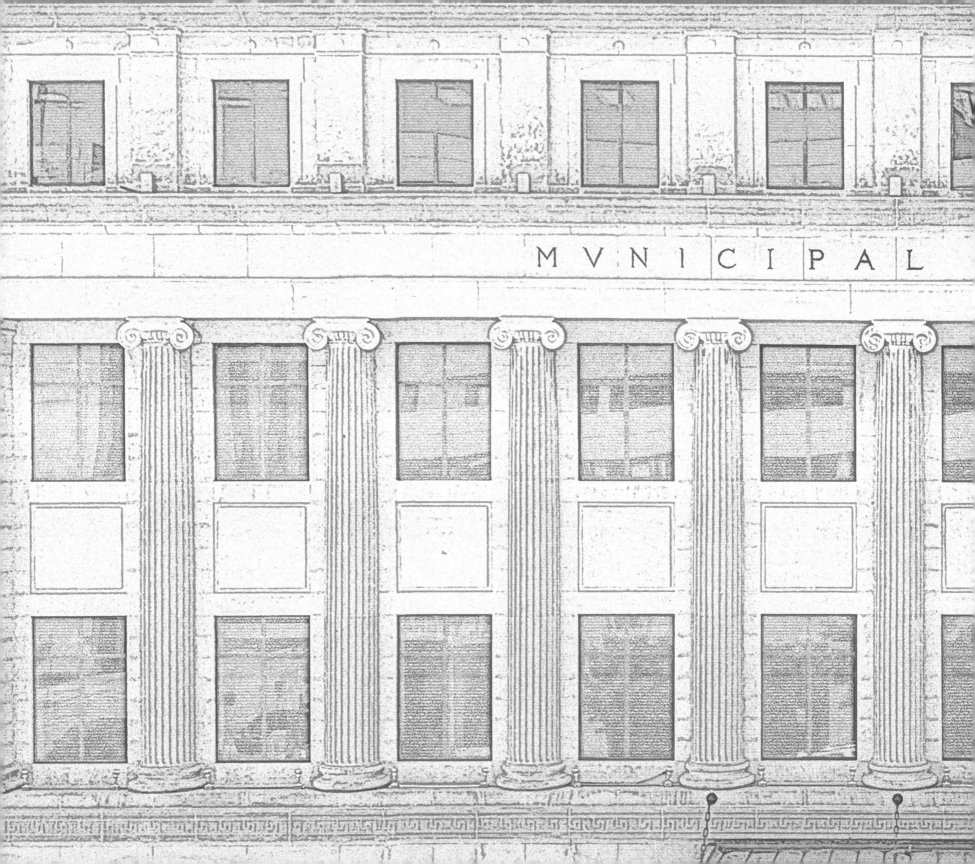

MVNICIPAL

Müllerhaus Publishing Arts, Inc.
DBA Müllerhaus Legacy
5200 South Yale Ave, Penthouse | Tulsa, Oklahoma 74135
MullerhausLegacy.com

Printed in Canada

21 20 19 18 17   1 2 3 4 5

ISBN: 978-0-9978410-3-9
LCCN: 2017913596

Cover and Interior Design by Douglas Miller / Müllerhaus Legacy

müllerhaus
[LEGACY]

THE CRAFT OF STORYTELLING. Great stories surround us. Every family, organization and community is steeped in memories of triumph and loss, sacrifice and love. But rarely are these stories woven together in a way that captivates this generation and inspires the next. That's where we can help. Whether on printed page or in digital media, Müllerhaus Legacy guides you in preserving and sharing your stories with a commitment that matches your passion. To be craftsmen in the trade of storytelling we've learned we must first be confidants in the art of listening. Our uncompromising standards of personal care, professional service and attention to detail will make your experience with us its own magnificent adventure.
Your stories are your legacy. Telling your stories is ours. | **MullerhausLegacy.com**

CONTENTS

x   *Acknowledgments*

xi   *Foreword*

xii   *Introduction*

SECTION ONE | TULSA'S QUEST *for* GOVERNANCE | *1894-1914*

2   CHAPTER 1   The Wild Years

12   CHAPTER 2   Taming the Magic City

22   CHAPTER 3   Regulating the Gusher

SECTION TWO | A TEMPLE *of* ACHIEVEMENT | *1914-1927*

36   CHAPTER 4   The Missing Piece

46   CHAPTER 5   Cleaning House

58   CHAPTER 6   Raising City Hall

SECTION THREE | ENDURING PRESTIGE | *1928-2017*

82   CHAPTER 7   Fifty Years of Service

102   CHAPTER 8   Love an Old Building

130   EPILOGUE   What Makes a City Hall?

135   *Notes*

138   *Index*

142   *Bibliography*

TULSA'S FIRST 40 MAYORS

Col. Edward E. *Calkins*
1st Mayor of Tulsa, 1898-1899

R.N. *Bynum*
2nd Mayor of Tulsa, 1899-1900

Lewis *Poe*
3rd Mayor of Tulsa, 1900-1901

George *Blakey*
4th Mayor of Tulsa, 1901-1903

Rev. George W. *Mowbray*
5th Mayor of Tulsa, 1903-1904

H.R. *Cline*
6th Mayor of Tulsa, 1904-1905

Dr. C.L. *Reeder*
7th Mayor of Tulsa, 1905-1906

John O. *Mitchell*
8th Mayor of Tulsa, 1906-1907
10th Mayor of Tulsa, 1909-1910

W.E. *Rohde*
9th Mayor of Tulsa, 1907-1909

Loyal J. *Martin*
11th Mayor of Tulsa, 1910-1912

Frank M. *Wooden*
12th Mayor of Tulsa, 1912-1916

John H. *Simmons*
13th Mayor of Tulsa, 1916-1918

Charles H. *Hubbard*
14th Mayor of Tulsa, 1918-1920

Thaddeus D. *Evans*
15th Mayor of Tulsa, 1920-1922

Herman F. *Newblock*
16th Mayor of Tulsa, 1922-1928
19th Mayor of Tulsa, 1932-1934

Daniel W. *Patton*
17th Mayor of Tulsa, 1928-1930

George L. *Watkins*
18th Mayor of Tulsa, 1930-1932

Dr. T.A. *Penney*
20th Mayor of Tulsa, 1934-1940

Clarence H. *Veale*
21st Mayor of Tulsa, 1940-1944

Olney F. *Flynn*
22nd Mayor of Tulsa, 1944-1946

Lee *Price* Jr.
23rd Mayor of Tulsa, 1946-1948

Roy B. *Lundy*
24th Mayor of Tulsa, 1948-1950

George H. *Stoner*
25th Mayor of Tulsa, 1950-1952

Clancy M. *Warren*
26th Mayor of Tulsa, 1952-1954

L.C. *Clark*
27th Mayor of Tulsa, 1954-1956

George E. *Norvell*
28th Mayor of Tulsa, 1956-1958

James L. *Maxwell*
29th Mayor of Tulsa, 1958-1966

James M. *Hewgley*
30th Mayor of Tulsa, 1966-1970

Robert J. *LaFortune*
31st Mayor of Tulsa, 1970-1978

James M. *Inhofe*
32nd Mayor of Tulsa, 1978-1984

Terry *Young*
33rd Mayor of Tulsa, 1984-1986

Dick *Crawford*
34th Mayor of Tulsa, 1986-1988

Rodger A. *Randle*
35th Mayor of Tulsa, 1988-1992

Susan *Savage*
36th Mayor of Tulsa, 1992-2002

Bill *LaFortune*
37th Mayor of Tulsa, 2002-2006

Kathy *Taylor*
38th Mayor of Tulsa, 2006-2009

Dewey F. *Bartlett* Jr.
39th Mayor of Tulsa, 2009-2016

G.T. *Bynum*
40th Mayor of Tulsa, 2016-

This BOOK *is* DEDICATED *to*
JOE COLEMAN & BRUCE ERVIN
WITHOUT WHOM WE WOULD HAVE EVEN LESS
of what LITTLE WE HAVE LEFT.

HAND-COLORED

Tulsa Municipal Building, 1919.   TULSA HISTORICAL SOCIETY

ACKNOWLEDGMENTS

MÜLLERHAUS LEGACY WOULD LIKE TO express their deepest appreciation to those who contributed time and resources to telling the story of Tulsa's Old City Hall Building. Specifically, thank you to Fred Dorwart, Skip B. Wolfe III, Jerry R. Nichols, Mayor Dewey F. Bartlett Jr., Tom Birmingham, S.M. Fallis, Beau Williams, Clayton Vaughn, the John Hope Center for Reconciliation, and the families of Joe Coleman and Bruce Ervin for access to their personal thoughts and memories. Thank you as well to Gilbert and Ellen Agronis, Joan Hoar, William Hellen, Nancy Schallner, and Mayor Bartlett for taking the time to read the manuscript in advance of publishing and for offering suggestions, corrections, and color.

Once again proving the ongoing value of Tulsa's outstanding historical society, we'd like to thank Archivist & Curator of Collections Ian Swärt and the generous staff of volunteers at the Tulsa Historical Society for their assistance in providing the majority of images that helped to bring this story to life. The survival of many of those images must be credited to the late Beryl Ford, and the Tulsa Jaycees, and Tulsa City-County Library who have made his collection accessible online.

High praise must be afforded to co-author John Hamill who helped extensively with the research, sidebars, feedback, interviews, and transcription necessary to produce this book. The editorial efforts of Jennifer Cyr, Nancy Kopper, and Christy Phillippe kept us all from looking bad.

When we started this project, we had no idea how much history was hiding behind the veil of those ten noble columns that front the Municipal Building. While this book only touches the high points, it certainly covers much more than originally expected. Through the many turns, the project's benefactor, Frederic Dorwart, current owner of the Old City Hall Building, remained engaged and encouraging, allowed us the time to work and the freedom to truly do our best. The ultimate credit for this project goes to him.

Tulsa Municipal Building, c.1935.

ONE HUNDRED YEARS AGO, Tulsa's shakers and movers saw the realization of their efforts to build a Municipal Building that represented the kind of city they intended to build. Today, Frederic Dorwart, Lawyers PLLC is honored to call that Municipal Building its home.

Inspired by John Bumgarner's magnificent book, *4th & Boston: Heart of the Magic Empire,* which celebrated 100 years of the heart of Downtown Tulsa, I asked that book's publisher, Douglas Miller with Müllerhaus Legacy, if he would write a small brochure for our centennial celebration of Old City Hall. Little did I expect this gem.

What particularly strikes me about the story of 100 years of Old City Hall is the primary role Tulsa's business and philanthropic communities have always contributed to the greatness of Tulsa. I hope you are as taken by the rich history of Tulsa's Municipal Building, and those who occupied it, as I am. We are proud to be a small part of the historic, ongoing, and future civic, economic, and social progress of Tulsa.

FREDERIC DORWART

Of NO SMALL IMPORT

"CIVIC LOVE FOR AN old landmark where thousands have dealt with matters concerning their lives and businesses is one of the intangibles that you can't have in a new building—it grows over decades."

— MARK ROSS, executive editor for the Arts Council of Tulsa, writing about the old Municipal Building in the October 1976 issue of the *Tulsalite*.

In response to the alarming rate at which Tulsa's Oil Boom architecture was being demolished in the late 1960s and early 1970s, this brass plaque, mounted on the 4th Street face of the Old City Hall Building in March of 1973, clearly states the architects' dedication to proving that historical preservation was a viable option for progressive development.

JOHN AMATUCCI

Erected 1917
Vacated 1969

Restored 1973

by

Coleman, Ervin & Assoc., Inc.
and
Nichols & Wolfe, Inc.

Dedicated to the Preservation
of Historic Landmarks and the
Beautification of Downtown

UNLESS THE INTENDED outcome is an engineering report, a real-estate appraisal, or a treatise on architecture, one cannot truly *tell the story* of a building without exploring the who, what, when, where, and especially, the *why* behind its creation. And how much more important are those qualifiers when telling the story of a public building—a place born to be of service to an entire community? Yet, when asked to create a book marking the centennial of Tulsa's Municipal Building on the southwest corner of 4th & Cincinnati in Tulsa, Oklahoma, I did not fully anticipate the depth of the task I was undertaking.

But I should have. The holistic relationship between people and architecture is not a new idea to me. Why, then, would an edifice intended to be a "fitting representation" of a city with such a remarkable and complex history not be imbued with its own act of the melodrama that is Tulsa?

I found so many allegorical parallels between Tulsa's quest for responsible governance and the

WHY WOULD *an* EDIFICE INTENDED *to be a* "FITTING REPRESENTATION" *of a* CITY *with* SUCH *a* REMARKABLE *and* COMPLEX HISTORY NOT BE IMBUED *with* ITS OWN ACT *of the* MELODRAMA THAT IS TULSA?

story of the Municipal Building that I felt this story must, at least partially, include the story of Tulsa's government. While most pioneer communities of that era walked the commonly accepted path of legally incorporating a city, then raising a building in which to run it, nothing in Tulsa came quite so easily. In the same way that responsible governance was late in coming to Tulsa, Tulsa's City Hall was also late in coming. Overlooked in the mad dash for oil boom riches; delayed by crime, corruption, and malfeasance; immediately outmoded by the very progress that built it; and then rescued by the economic collapse that brought its city to its knees, the Municipal Building is as steeped in irony as is the Magic City itself.

Abandoned and left for dead after its first fifty years of government service, it barely escaped demolition to then spend its second fifty years in the private sector in a way that still serves the community it was built to represent. At one hundred years old, the Municipal Building is more than just another repurposed office building. It is, in fact, *the* repurposed office building, which stood as the first bulwark against the wrecking ball of Urban Renewal to become the birthplace of the preservation movement that secured the future of Tulsa's now-celebrated oil boom-era architecture.

Contemplating these two very different half-centuries of the Municipal Building's history, I can't help but wonder what the next hundred years has in store for both our resilient Old City Hall, and the city that birthed it. While each town has a history worth remembering and every old building has a few good stories to tell, not many towns have a history quite like Tulsa's, and even fewer buildings have more stories to tell. When some future historian updates Tulsa's biography in the year 2117, I fully expect that it will still be a remarkable story about a good place filled with good people who have pride in their community and a hunger for both justice and prosperity. I also fully expect that the two-hundred-year-old Municipal Building will still be playing a part of no small import.

— *Douglas Miller*

1st City Hall
(1836-1861)

The Creek Council Oak Tree

18th & Cheyenne. As an appropriate reminder that Tulsa did not begin with the arrival of the railroad, **J.M. Hall** *(left)*, the man credited as the founder of modern Tulsa, visits the ancient Creek Council Oak, c.1921. Hall is joined by Tulsa Oilman, **Charles B. Peters** *(center)*, who owned the property at the time, and **Col. Clarence B. Douglas** *(right)*, the author of Tulsa's first history book.

It was the Muscogee (Creek) Loachapoka Tallasi people who first established a functional local government here when they lit their ceremonial fire beneath this great tree in 1836 following their forced removal from their native lands in the East.

Tulsa Historical Society

"It is 'The Tulsa Spirit'
that has OVERCOME ALMOST INSURMOUNTABLE DIFFICULTIES,
DEFEATED ALL OPPOSITION, DEFIED ALL LOCAL DISASTERS and, UNAFRAID,
FACED the FUTURE with CONFIDENCE and DETERMINATION to SUCCEED.
It is this 'TULSA SPIRIT,' the CONTROLLING IMPULSE of MORE THAN
100,000 PEOPLE, that LOOKS the FUTURE in the EYE and SAYS,
'Tulsa Will!'"

FROM PAGE NINETEEN

TULSA'S
QUEST *for* GOVERNANCE

MVNICIPAL BVILDING

The
WILD YEARS

ANDREW PERRYMAN HAD BEEN on one of his infamous tears for three sol-id days before accidentally killing himself in a spectacular fashion while the whole town watched. The drama unfolded along Tulsa's Main Street on All Hallows' Eve 1894. The incident was reported in newspapers across the region, which was somewhat unusual given the profligate character of Tulsa's early days. An intoxicated troublemaker meeting a violent end was so common in the rowdy little village that the incident might never have garnered special attention had Andrew Perryman not been a member of one of the region's most noble families and the son of the chief of the Creek Nation—and had he not

2ND CITY HALL (1882-1897)
Hall & Co. Store

Northeast corner of 1st & Main. Although Tulsa's first official City Hall would have to wait until incorporation came in 1897, the Hall & Co. store filled the need for a place where Tulsa's early planters, both Indian and settler, could plan and dream about the future potential of their rowdy little cowtown.

J.M. Hall *(white shirt standing to the right of the center pole)* poses with his friend and advocate, Creek native George Perryman *(left side of pole)* on the front porch of the Hall & Co. Store, c.1890.
TULSA HISTORICAL SOCIETY

J.M. HALL
FOUNDING FATHER *of* MODERN TULSA

J.M. Hall came to Tulsa as an employee of his older brother Harry C. Hall in the summer of 1882. Harry held a construction contract laying rails across Indian Territory for the Frisco Railroad that ended at the Arkansas River. Deciding to put down roots at the last depot before the river, the brothers selected the site for Tulsa and worked tirelessly to grow their nascent town into a place with promise. Harry Hall died in 1895 leaving the tasking of raising Tulsa to J.M., their fellow pioneers, and the Creek Indians who had established businesses and located their families there. Over the course of his long life, J.M. contributed directly to founding Tulsa Public Schools, The University of Tulsa, First Presbyterian Church of Tulsa, and the Tulsa Regional Chamber of Commerce.

TULSA HISTORICAL SOCIETY

1890

Cummins   St. Louis,

taken one of Tulsa's most beloved citizens with him to the grave.

The twenty-one-year-old Perryman, along with a group of friends and fellow Creek Indians, had been drunk and disorderly for days. But the trouble in town didn't start until the group ran across a gathering of boys near the train depot. Perryman was said to have taken a few shots at the boys' toes just for the pleasure of seeing them jump. Then, vowing to "shoot up Main Street," he and his friends stumbled over to the front porch of the Hall & Company store on the northwest corner of 1st & Main Streets. The porch at this establishment was a popular gathering place and Tulsa's unofficial center of business and society. The proprietor of the store was J.M. Hall, a cordial shopkeeper considered by his peers to be the founding father of modern Tulsa. As was so often the case in such situations—of which there were many—the town had little more to rely on than Hall's amiable and calming nature to defuse potentially violent situations. On this day, however, despite Hall's best efforts to reason with the young men, Perryman and his friends proceeded to make Main Street their personal shooting gallery in a demonstration of drunken marksmanship that went on until the group ran out of ammunition.

Across Main Street and a little north from Hall & Company's front porch stood a hardware and dry goods shop called the Archer Store. Established by an orphaned, mixed-blood Cherokee named Thomas Jefferson "Jeff" Archer, the store was credited by the modest Mr. Hall as being Tulsa's first business. Truthfully, both Archer and Hall set up their shops at about the

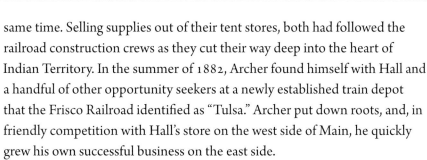

same time. Selling supplies out of their tent stores, both had followed the railroad construction crews as they cut their way deep into the heart of Indian Territory. In the summer of 1882, Archer found himself with Hall and a handful of other opportunity seekers at a newly established train depot that the Frisco Railroad identified as "Tulsa." Archer put down roots, and, in friendly competition with Hall's store on the west side of Main, he quickly grew his own successful business on the east side.

It was into the Archer Store that Andrew Perryman staggered in search of shells to reload his six-shooter. Archer and Perryman were known to be friends, but when Archer tried to talk the inebriated Perryman out of reloading his gun, Perryman threatened to kill him. Archer sternly reminded Perryman of their friendship and assured him that Perryman wouldn't want to kill a friend. Stories differ as to what exactly happened next, but all sources agree that Perryman somehow ended up with a loaded gun. And then, whether accidentally or on purpose, he fired several shots inside the store, one of which hit the supply of black powder that Archer kept in kegs beneath the front counter. A series of three nearly simultaneous explosions lifted the roof and blew out the side of the building. Archer was thrown through the heavy merchandise shelves along the side wall. In addition to the concussive damage his body took from the blast, his clothes also caught fire. He immediately freed himself from the wreckage, then proceeded to run down

THE PERRYMAN FAMILY
TULSA'S FIRST FAMILY

Out of all the names one might associate with criminality in Tulsa, Perryman was not one of them. Andrew Perryman's family—his father, Chief Legus Perryman *(pictured right)*, along with his aunt and uncle, George and "Aunt Rachel" Perryman, were not only pillars in the community, but Tulsa itself could not have existed without their leadership and blessings. The Perryman family, deeply invested in ranching, benefited tremendously from the coming of the railroad which provided them with badly needed access to cattle markets. They befriended J.M. Hall and the other pioneers and used their Indian land rights to secure property for the settlers to establish homes and businesses in Tulsa.

BERYL FORD COLLECTION

Main Street, consumed in a plume of smoke and fire. Perryman, having received the full force of the blast, was blown upward through the ceiling. He was eventually found on what was left of the roof. His body was so badly burned, lacerated, and broken that he was nearly unrecognizable. Within hours, he was dead.

Although Archer survived the initial explosion, his wounds also proved to be fatal. While friends and family gathered at his bedside, he lingered on in desperate agony at his home near Main & Easton for just over a month. But in early December of 1894, thirty-three-year-old Jeff Archer finally succumbed to his injuries, leaving behind two children—ages three and one—a wife who was five months pregnant, and a town utterly heartbroken.[1]

THE INCIDENT at the Archer Store epitomized Tulsa's early struggle with lawlessness and its lack of effective governance. Yet it was also steeped in the kind of irony that bestowed upon Tulsa its unlikely and fascinating beginnings. The town's dusty main street and few hundred residents were no strangers to death and violence. As demonstrated by the way in which a drunken son of the nation's leader and his friends could so brazenly terrorize the town and remain unchallenged by anything stronger than the calming words of a shopkeeper, Tulsa needed the kind of law and order that could only come from an authoritative hand of reliable governance if it was to have any hope for a livable future.

Tulsa was within the boundaries of the Creek Nation, which meant that tribal government was, in theory, responsible for keeping the peace. But the problem of establishing law and order could not, in fairness, be laid at the feet of the Creek government. The problem was more systemic in nature. Insomuch as the tribe tried to police their own territory, their ability to do so was limited by restrictions the United States government had placed on them. The Creeks, like all of the Five Nations, could only rely on small detachments of "lighthorsemen" for law enforcement. While tribal courts and their officers only enjoyed criminal jurisdiction over their own citizens, it was estimated that, by 1894, non-Indian United States citizens outnumbered official tribal populations nearly three to one.[2] The consequence of this unfortunate ratio was a land of lawlessness where bandits, debtors, convicts, and deserters could, for the most part, escape the hand of justice.

The United States Congress responded to the lawlessness of Indian Territory by first expanding the jurisdiction of U.S. District Courts in Arkansas, Texas, and Kansas. Then, beginning in 1889, it established federal courts inside Indian Territory, first in Muskogee, then in McAlester and Ardmore. Although the territory was vast and the outlaws were many, federal judges were well-armed with an army of courageous, daring, and determined United States deputy marshals who eventually brought a semblance of law and order to Indian Territory. Clashes between lawmen and outlaws in the wilds around Tulsa created legends on both sides of the law.

Three U.S. deputy marshals became so well-known for their dogmatic pursuit of justice that they earned the unofficial title of the "Three Guardsmen." William "Bill" Tilghman, Chris Madsen, and Henry "Heck" Thomas were credited with ending the careers—fatally, when necessary—of more than three hundred of the territory's most vicious and brutal outlaws. As an acknowledgment of both their tenacity and their high regard for fairness, ethics, and justice, the outlaws themselves gave them the title of "guardsmen."[3]

Such overtures of respect might seem unlikely, given the brutal nature of Western outlawry, but most of the gangs and their leaders lived by certain unspoken codes of conduct. While this was common across most of the West, it was infamously true in Tulsa. For all the trouble the little village had with drunks, gamblers, and pursuers of vice, the "professional" outlaws remained generally peaceful when they were in town, and they never targeted Tulsa's

bank, its businesses, or trains. Without enjoying the benefit of reliable law enforcement, the good people of Tulsa realized early on that offering the accommodation of a blind eye to the outlaws' malefactions in exchange for the town's security was ultimately best for everyone. Thus, seeing Tulsa as a "safe harbor" where they could resupply without being reported or arrested, a good many outlaws— Belle Starr, the Youngers, the Dalton Gang, and likely many others—established hideouts within a day's ride of town. In some cases, the asylum of Tulsa grew to be respected by lawmen who would have jumped at the opportunity to bag their quarry anywhere else. In fact, the members of one of the territory's most infamous gangs, the Daltons, even shared a Sunday morning house of worship with one of the territory's most aggressive and dogmatic lawmen.[4]

U.S. Deputy Marshal Bill Tilghman, a close personal friend of Wyatt Earp, was a city marshal in Dodge City, Kansas, prior to becoming one of the "Three Guardsmen."

Known as the "Great Dane," Danish immigrant **Chris Madsen** also served in the Fifth Cavalry and in Roosevelt's Rough Riders. He was later appointed Chief of Police for Oklahoma City.

U.S. Deputy Marshal Henry "Heck" Thomas. After helping to rid the territory of the Daltons and Doolins, Thomas served for seven years as Lawton's police chief.

Surprisingly, Grat, Bob, and Emmet Dalton regularly attended Tulsa's First Methodist-Episcopal Church, which stood on the west side of Main Street, near present-day Cameron. During the same period, between 1888 and 1891, one of the Three Guardsmen, U.S. Deputy Marshal Heck Thomas, came to Tulsa as often as he was able, and attended the same Methodist-Episcopal church while there. According to Hannah Mowbray, the wife of the church's minister, Reverend George W. Mowbray, the misdeeds of the Dalton Gang during that time were well-known: "They sang in my husband's church on Sunday and ravaged the country during the week," she revealed many years after the fact.

ALTHOUGH HECK THOMAS *had* BOLDLY FACED DEATH COUNTLESS TIMES OVER *the* COURSE *of* HIS CAREER, *it* SEEMS HE *had* MET HIS MATCH *in the* REVEREND MOWBRAY.

Heck Thomas usually stayed in the home of Reverend Mowbray while he was in Tulsa. Although their professions were very different, the deputy and the clergyman had much in common. George and Hannah were two of the most indomitable personalities in early Tulsa, and they did much to strengthen the hand of right and justice within the community. Reverend Mowbray found himself enamored by Heck's tales of danger and adventure. He was also, no doubt, inspired by Heck's reputation for stopping at no end to bring a man to justice. But unbeknownst to the Mowbrays, it was not Heck's affection for the clergyman and his wife that kept him tied to Tulsa.

Heck Thomas had met the Mowbrays in the summer of 1888, just two months after they took over the pulpit of Tulsa's little Methodist church. Heck had been stuck in town while recovering from gunshot wounds he had suffered in an ambush that had occurred just east of present-day Sapulpa. During their chance meeting, Heck, who was thirty-eight at the time, was charmed by the Mowbrays' beautiful fifteen-year-old daughter, Matie. His affections were reciprocated, but it wasn't until Matie turned eighteen, in 1891, that their intentions were finally revealed by Heck's marriage proposal.

The Mowbray Family shortly after their arrival in Tulsa, 1888. Rev. George W. Mowbray, Matie standing at left, Annie standing at right, youngest daughter Grace front row center, and Hannah Mowbray at right.

It is hard to say whether Reverend Mowbray was more upset by a forty-one-year-old man proposing to his eighteen-year-old daughter or if he was angered by the realization that the famous Heck Thomas hadn't really been coming all the way to Tulsa to enjoy George's personal company. Either way, George and Hannah Mowbray refused to give their blessing to the proposal and insisted there would be no wedding.

The Mowbrays had become legends for their intractable cogency in the face of even the most rigorous trials. And although Heck Thomas had boldly faced death countless times over the course of his career, it seems he had met his match in the Reverend Mowbray. Instead of contesting the issue face-to-face with Mowbray, the otherwise courageous lawman slipped out the back door with his young bride-to-be in tow. In October 1891, Heck and Matie eloped and were married in Arkansas City, Kansas.[5]

Matie was the Mowbrays' second daughter. Their eldest, Annie, was already married and had an infant daughter by the time Matie left town with Heck. Unlike Matie's union with Heck, Annie's marriage had been wholeheartedly blessed by her parents. The man whom Annie had wed was one of Tulsa's founding citizens, loved by all and recognized in the business community "for [his] honesty and manly principles."[6] As a husband and a father, he was described as "one whose every word and action in their happy home was love and kindness."[7] Thus was Annie's husband described in his obituary—the obituary of none other than Jeff Archer. Annie (Mowbray) Archer was the pregnant mother of two who had been widowed by the explosion at the Archer Store. She never remarried, opting instead to live with George and Hannah in the big, beautiful house she would have shared with Jeff.

George and Hannah Mowbray's two eldest daughters were teenagers when the family moved to Tulsa in 1888. Annie (left) married Jeff Archer. Matie (right) married Heck Thomas. BERYL FORD COLLECTION

AT THE time his brother-in-law had been killed in Tulsa, Heck Thomas and his fellow guardsmen, Tilghman and Madsen, were crisscrossing the Twin Territories in pursuit of the Wild Bunch—a deadly amalgamation of the surviving members of the Doolin and Dalton Gangs. Before setting out after the Wild Bunch, Thomas had assisted Tilghman in bringing peace to the town of Perry, across the border in Oklahoma Territory. Perry was a wild boomtown of more than twenty-five thousand people that had been formed in a single day following the Cherokee Strip Land Run of 1893. Perry was so violent and vice-ridden that it quickly—and justifiably—earned the title of "Hell's Half-Acre." Thomas and Tilghman had been given temporary leave from their roles as U.S. deputy marshals to accept positions as town marshals that were eagerly offered to them by Perry's first mayor, John M. Brogan. As reported by the *Perry Daily Times*, within just a few months, "there was a 'cleaning up' by the police force, which gradually pushed out the vicious element—or at least drove it under cover."[8] In fact, the reason Tilghman and Thomas had been available to pivot to the Wild Bunch campaign in the spring of 1894 was that the town council had ultimately fired them due to the loss of revenue and population that resulted from their effectiveness.[9]

One can only assume that, back in Tulsa, the heartbroken Mowbrays were pondering how the vice and violence that had taken the life of one son-in-law might have been prevented by the other. During the twelve years that Tulsa had existed as a small cowtown and trading post with a few hundred residents, it had been plagued by persistent vice and disorder. Yet, working with only four deputies, Thomas and Tilghman had managed to clean up a city twenty-five times the size of Tulsa, a city that had had problems far greater, and they did so in less than six months.

As bad as Tulsa's problems were, however, the town also had many stalwart citizens who earnestly wanted the little village to grow into a place of decency with moral conviction and promise. Reverend Mowbray, for his part, did as much as any man of the cloth could do. Not only did he regularly and passionately preach against the "wiles of the devil," but after one particularly raucous evening of fighting, shooting, and revelry enacted by area cowboys, Mowbray went out alone to confront the ranchers who employed them. In his centennial history of Tulsa's First United Methodist Church, *The First Hundred,* Wishard Lemons described the scene: "With all the dignity he could muster, which was considerable, [Mowbray] spoke sternly to [the ranchers.] He told them that except for the grace of God innocent citizens could be killed. With his powerful preaching voice … he said, 'In the name of God, gentlemen, this must cease at once!'"[10]

The MOWBRAYS PONDERED HOW *the* VICE *and* VIOLENCE *that had* TAKEN *the* LIFE *of* ONE SON-IN-LAW MIGHT *have been* PREVENTED *by the* OTHER.

According to Lemons, the confrontation worked, insomuch as that it solved most of the problems around Mowbray's church. But it was no more of a solution for Tulsa than the calming words of the amiable Mr. Hall in his mercantile. Unlike Tulsa, the town of Perry had the ability to form a city council, to levy taxes, and to hire a police force. Being under the jurisdiction of the Creek Nation, Tulsa had no such ability. But within months of the Archer Store incident, the federal government would start handing down a series of highly controversial decisions that would bring dramatic change to Indian Territory. And Reverend Mowbray was determined to be at the center of the changes that promised to redefine Tulsa.

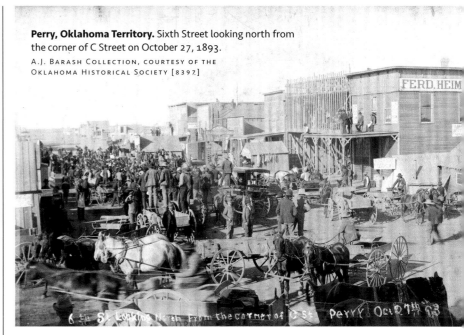

Perry, Oklahoma Territory. Sixth Street looking north from the corner of C Street on October 27, 1893.
A.J. BARASH COLLECTION, COURTESY OF THE OKLAHOMA HISTORICAL SOCIETY [8397]

First City Officers of Perry, Oklahoma Territory, November 1, 1893. Acting Town Marshal Heck Thomas is standing the fifth from the left.
OKLAHOMA HISTORICAL SOCIETY PHOTOGRAPH COLLECTION, COURTESY OF THE OKLAHOMA HISTORICAL SOCIETY [4032]

TAMING *the* MAGIC CITY

AFTER THE DEATH OF HIS son-in-law, Reverend Mowbray retired from the ministry to take over operations at the Archer Store. Not only was he providing for his wife, Hannah, and their youngest daughter, but he had also become the breadwinner for Annie and the three children she had with Jeff. Moving from ministry to business gave Mowbray more incentive than just moral diligence alone to set about the development of a town. ¶ Mowbray, along with Tulsa's other progressive leaders, would not wait long for the dramatic change they had been hoping for. In the spring of 1895, the United States Congress passed a series of aggressive and sweeping legislative actions[1]

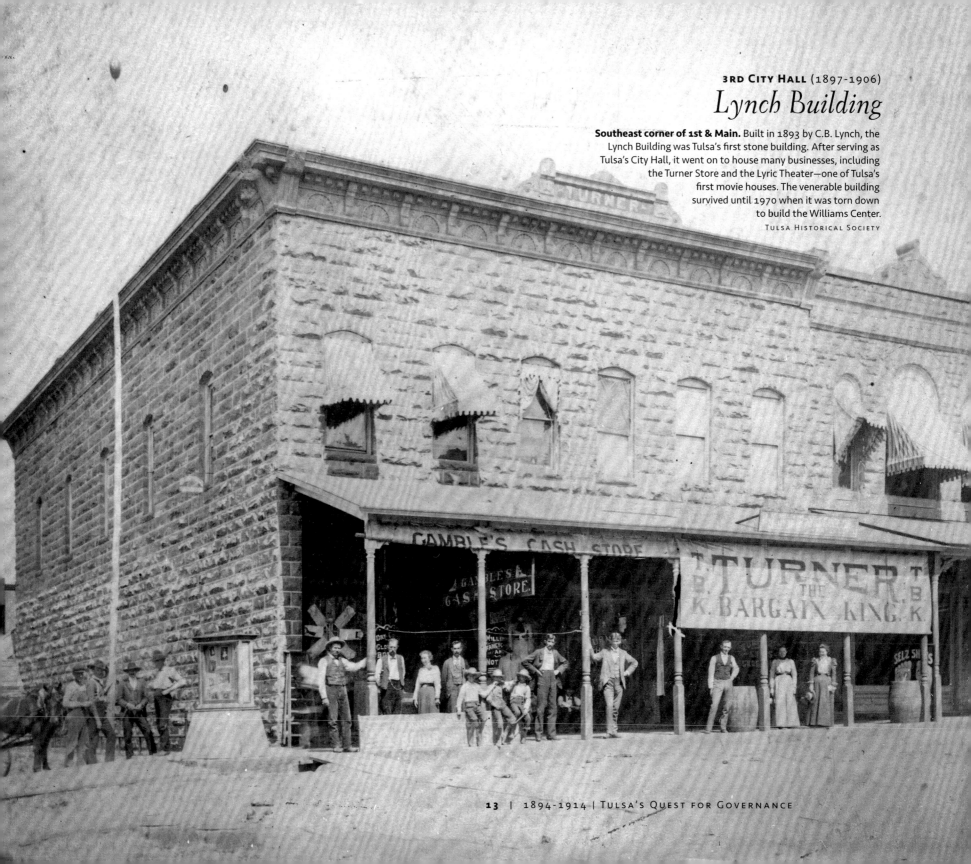

3RD CITY HALL (1897-1906)

Lynch Building

Southeast corner of 1st & Main. Built in 1893 by C.B. Lynch, the Lynch Building was Tulsa's first stone building. After serving as Tulsa's City Hall, it went on to house many businesses, including the Turner Store and the Lyric Theater—one of Tulsa's first movie houses. The venerable building survived until 1970 when it was torn down to build the Williams Center.

TULSA HISTORICAL SOCIETY

Reverend Mowbray with his extended family in 1902 on the front porch of the Archer house at 524 North Main. *Front Row:* Beth Thomas, Harley Thomas, Grace Winterringer, Mildred Winterringer, Helen Mowbray, Hannah Elizabeth Mowbray holding baby Madeline Mowbray, Gertrude Winterringer, George W. Mowbray Sr., Melton Winterringer, Georgia Archer, Annie Archer and James V. Archer. *Back Row:* Heck Thomas, Matie Thomas, George W. Mowbray Jr., Mame Mowbray, Mabel G. Archer. BERYL FORD COLLECTION

that all but swept away tribal self-government across Indian Territory. Among the many changes forced upon the Five Nations, Congress had opened a pathway for non-tribal members to own land within Indian Territory and gave towns within tribal jurisdictions the right to incorporate.[2] Tulsa would have the opportunity to evolve from a mere population center and trading post to an actual legal entity, with the ability to write municipal law and levy the taxes needed to build schools, streets, and sidewalks, and of course, establish law enforcement.

Although Tulsa stood at the dawn of a new age, its wild years had no intention of passing quietly into the night. In the early morning hours of December 5, 1897, fire swept the east side of Main between 1st and 2nd Streets. Uncontested by anything more substantial than desperate townsfolk with buckets of water, the blaze devoured almost the entire block containing Tulsa's newest and best-built stone structures—including the only bank. Upon receiving word of the event, *The Baxter Springs News* breathlessly reported, "The town of Tulsa, I.T., was very nearly wiped off the face of the earth."[3] While it wasn't *that* bad, the event surely hardened the resolve of town fathers and likely gave the need for a fire department equal billing with their need for law enforcement.

In the immediate aftermath of what came to be known as the "Great Fire of 1897," a young attorney named Harry Campbell was given the task of writing Tulsa's petition of incorporation. With Campbell's document in hand, a provisional committee led by J.M. Hall, which also included Reverend Mowbray, Dr. Sam Kennedy, Prior Price, Tate Brady, L.M. Poe, R.E. Lynch, Colonel Edward Calkins, and J.D. Seaman, loaded up in buggies for the long and rough ride to the federal court in Muskogee. The next day, January 18, 1898, Judge William R. Springer signed Tulsa's official Charter of Incorporation.[4] Thus, sixteen years after the Frisco Railroad had located the depot it called "Tulsa," and sixty-two years after the Loachapoka Tallasi people of the Muscogee (Creek) Nation had established the first village in the area, the City of Tulsa was officially born.

WITH INCORPORATION, Tulsa had the ability to establish a legal government, write municipal codes, empower a court, and levy the taxes

needed to fund the improvements and services the people so badly needed. The first order of business, however, was electing the body that would lead this new government.

Tulsa's first town council was comprised of a mayor, city attorney, city engineer, city clerk, police judge, chief of police, and five at-large aldermen known as "free holders." Colonel Edward Calkins became the city's first mayor, and Wess Kennedy the first city marshal.[6]

Looking north on Main Street from 2nd Street at about the time Tulsa became a city.
BERYL FORD COLLECTION

On the eve of Tulsa's incorporation, this dismal observation on the state of the community was printed by Tulsa's *Indian Republican* newspaper. "The *Indian Republican* believes that a better and brighter day has thus dawned for Tulsa. Conditions had become intolerable here and something had to be done. When the United States commission, especially a high-class jurist like Judge Elijah Tollett, is forced to leave Tulsa because of fear of his life at the hands of a band of outlaws, when it is not safe at night to light up a store or residence without having that light shot out, when stores are blown up and their proprietor, one of our foremost citizens, killed as was Jeff Archer, and some fronts broken out as was Tate Brady's, when our kangaroo city marshal, (chosen by the vigilance committee), Tom Stufflebeam, gets drunk and falls in the river and would have been drowned if it had not been for Burl Cox, when bands of outlaws roam the hills on every side of town, it's time good citizens who expect to build a city here and raise their families, rise in their might and assert their rights."[5]

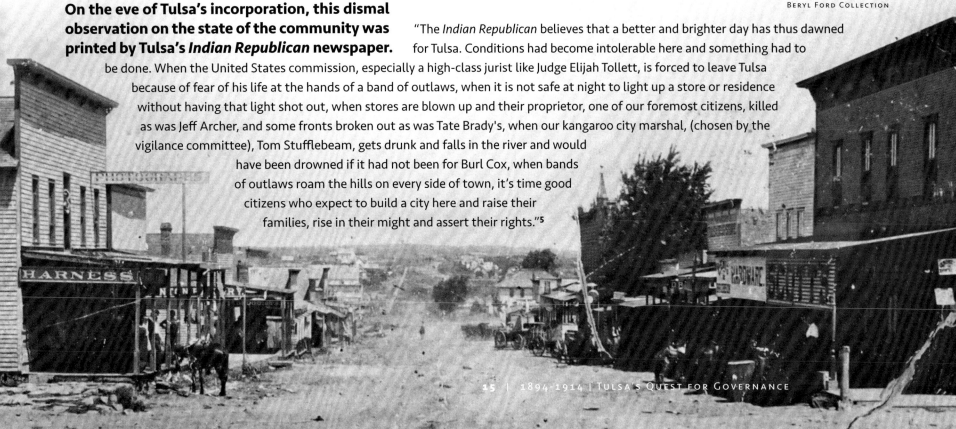

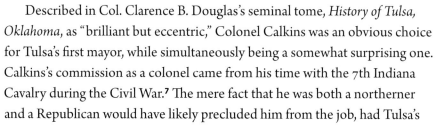

Described in Col. Clarence B. Douglas's seminal tome, *History of Tulsa, Oklahoma,* as "brilliant but eccentric," Colonel Calkins was an obvious choice for Tulsa's first mayor, while simultaneously being a somewhat surprising one. Calkins's commission as a colonel came from his time with the 7th Indiana Cavalry during the Civil War.[7] The mere fact that he was both a northerner and a Republican would have likely precluded him from the job, had Tulsa's Democratic founding fathers not been concerned, at that point, with matters more practical than partisan politics. Because the first mayor would be responsible for the creation of a government from scratch, the choice of Calkins made sense. At sixty-one years of age, he was considerably older and more experienced than all but a few of Tulsa's founders. He had knowledge of the law, administrative experience, and leadership qualities. In reference to his presence and gravitas, J.M. Hall once observed, "When the Colonel was wound up for [a] speech, the oratory attracted considerable attention."[8]

Colonel Calkins was an attorney by profession. According to Hall, he was Tulsa's first. At the time of incorporation, Tulsa had only four lawyers, all of whom, including Calkins, had arrived at about the same time. In April of 1895, a United States Commissioners Court was established in Tulsa, with Judge Elijah G. Tollett Jr. presiding. Once word began to spread that Tulsa would have its own court, Colonel Calkins became the first to ride into town in pursuit of the opportunity the court would create for those in the legal profession. Over the next year and a half, Calkins was followed by Flowers Nelson, Harry Campbell, and L.M. Poe, who would become Tulsa's third mayor in 1900.

COLONEL
EDWARD E. CALKINS

1st MAYOR *of* TULSA [1898-1899]

EDWARD CALKINS WAS BORN into a prominent and politically active family in Fulton County, Indiana, on August 20, 1836. He was educated at Ohio Wesleyan University, at Delaware, Ohio, and read law for three years at Greenville, Ohio, where he was admitted to the practice of law in 1860.

At the onset of the Civil War, Calkins received a commission as a major with the 87th Ohio Volunteers. In his third month of duty, he was taken prisoner at the Battle of Harpers Ferry. Subsequently released in a prisoner exchange, he re-enlisted with the 7th Indiana Cavalry where he received the rank of colonel but lost his right hand.

After the war, Calkins established a law practice in Rochester, Indiana, served two years in the Indiana state legislature, then, in 1889, headed west to Indian Territory in search of opportunity and adventure. His 1894 arrival in Tulsa made him the town's first attorney which contributed to his appointment as the city's first mayor just four years later. J.M. Hall credited Calkins as, "an enthusiastic Tulsa booster" following his active participation as a speaker for the town on the 1908 train tour. Calkins, with his wife Eleanor, did well in real estate and spent the rest of their lives in Tulsa. Calkins died in Tulsa at age 73 on May 3, 1911.

Hall, well-known for his fidelity to the Democratic Party, was likely able to forgive Colonel Calkins for his Republicanism, because, like Hall, Calkins was also a Presbyterian. And for as much as Hall loved his politics, he loved his church more. A shared passion for faith and politics was common among Tulsa's founding citizens, and due to the efforts of Hall, the Presbyterians were the most influential church body in the village. Regardless of denomination, however, nearly all of Tulsa's early pioneers—including the Methodist Reverend Mowbray—cast their lot with the Democrats. The most obvious and outspoken exception was Dr. Sam Kennedy, the pioneer medical practitioner who settled in Tulsa in 1891 having yet to treat his first patient. Kennedy went on to make his fortune in oil

and build the Kennedy Building at 4th & Boston, the same location where he hosted Tulsa's first Republican convention in 1900.

Fortunately for Tulsa's small but active handful of Republicans, municipal elections stayed nonpartisan until after Oklahoma became a state in 1907. That's not to say that politics were not a lively affair in Tulsa's early years. But then, as now, the value of partisanship at the local level proved to be more of an obstruction to progress than any practical advantage to the candidate— or the city. As Nina Lane Dunn explained in her book, *Tulsa's Magic Roots*, "By reading the newspapers of that era, it becomes apparent that politics had more-or-less to do with the charges and countercharges hurled about as to where the responsibility for the lack of law enforcement lay."[9] Even on that front, she went on to explain, "Those who were strongest for law enforcement formed nonpartisan tickets."[10]

Regardless of which political party was in charge, the real power and influence in the newly incorporated city didn't come with political parties. In fact, it didn't reside with Tulsa's official governing body at all. Right from the beginning, forming a government was a means to an end. And that end was commerce.

IN 1901, oil was discovered in the neighboring town of Red Fork across the Arkansas River from Tulsa. Although actual production from Red Fork turned out to be quite modest in comparison to the mighty Glenn Pool discovery that would transform the entire region just four years later, it was enough to give everyone their first real taste of success. It was a taste the optimistic men of Tulsa liked—and they wanted more of it. A lot more.

Competition for commerce and the prestige that came with it was stiff between the developing towns throughout Indian Territory. So much so that before oil was discovered, the men of Tulsa held Muskogee in outright contempt. Even the graciously amicable J.M.

Hall admitted, "The real pioneers of Tulsa had no love for Muskogee, the city that monopolized federal offices in the early days, greatly inconveniencing Tulsa business and professional men."[11] The explosion of growth that would come from the oil industry was, in a way, Tulsa's revenge on Muskogee, as men there were left, as Hall said many years later, "sitting and waiting for that city to grow to Tulsa's size."[12] But once opportunity presented itself in neighboring Red Fork, it was Tulsa that assumed the role of the aggressor, angling to relieve that community from the burden of its good fortune.

The Red Fork discovery took Muskogee out of Tulsans' minds (for a little while, at least), as it focused competitive intensity among the towns connected by the Frisco Railroad—Sapulpa, Red Fork, and Tulsa. Of the three towns, Tulsa was at the greatest disadvantage, because it was located on the opposite side of the Arkansas River from Red Fork's oil field. Although isolated and having only a narrow railroad bridge and unreliable ferry service, Tulsa had in spades a resource other communities lacked—a very real factor the city fathers called the "Tulsa Spirit"—a "dominating dynamic force directing and controlling the destiny of Tulsa." [13]

It is said that between ambition and opportunity, the former is the greater part of success. And in Indian Territory, no one seemed able to match the seemingly limitless ambition of the early pioneers, who were hell-bent on making something out of Tulsa. Certain names appear on virtually every document and in every story that led Tulsa down the path to becoming what would soon be called a "Magic City." Paramount among these names was, of course, J.M. Hall, followed by others like Mowbray, Kennedy, Bynum, Forsythe, Brady, and Lynch. As Tulsa continued to develop, many more names that personified the Tulsa Spirit were added to the ranks of the "Tulsa Boosters," as they called themselves.

Rightly identifying this ambitious spirit in his fellow boosters, and seeing the opportunity to cash in on Red Fork's good fortune, Hall called for the formation of the Commercial Club, predecessor of today's Tulsa Regional Chamber of Commerce. Almost from the moment it was formed, the Commercial Club would prove to be as great of an asset to both the development of Tulsa and the long-term sustainability of its community,

In its best attempt to explain "Tulsa Spirit" to the outsiders who would be mobbing the city for the International Petroleum Exposition and Congress in 1923, the Chamber of Commerce printed the following:[14]

"It is 'The Tulsa Spirit' that HAS OVERCOME ALMOST INSURMOUNTABLE DIFFICULTIES, DEFEATED ALL OPPOSITION, DEFIED ALL LOCAL DISASTERS and, UNAFRAID, FACED the FUTURE with CONFIDENCE and DETERMINATION to SUCCEED. It is this 'TULSA SPIRIT,' the CONTROLLING IMPULSE of MORE THAN 100,000 PEOPLE, that LOOKS the FUTURE in the EYE and SAYS, 'Tulsa Will!'"

culture, and diversified economy as the oil that funded it.

To lead an organization focused on both economic growth and community development, there was surely no more ideal booster than a strong-willed man with unimpeachable character and the firsthand understanding that a community needs economic opportunity, a moral center, and a government with the strength to protect the good from the bad. Thus, in 1901, the Commercial Club formed under its first president, Reverend G.W. Mowbray.

REVEREND
GEORGE W. MOWBRAY
5th MAYOR of TULSA [1903-1904]

PHYSICALLY STOUT IN THE manner of successful men of his time, the Rev. George W. Mowbray was the equal to a number of successful men as a minister, merchant, and mayor—among other pursuits.

Born in Melton, Leicestershire, in 1847, this Englishman was a Methodist minister sent from Kansas to Tulsa in 1888 to revive its fledgling Methodist church that had fallen on hard times. He, and his wife Hannah, revitalized the church to the tune of counting the Dalton Boys as members of the church choir. When the Presbyterian-sponsored school faced overcrowding, he opened a second Tulsa school. Later, he was called to missionary work in Oklahoma, but rushed back to Tulsa to assume responsibility for his daughter Anna's family after her husband, Thomas Jefferson Archer, was killed in the tragic Archer Store incident of 1894.

Mowbray left the ministry to run the store, then studied to become an undertaker, established a funeral home that served Tulsa's community for many years, and along the way served as Tulsa's first public school board president. While serving as the founding president of Tulsa's Commercial Club, the forerunner of the Chamber of Commerce, Mowbray helped negotiate favorable railroad alignments that greatly impacted Tulsa's future success. He also managed a realty company, and served as Tulsa's fifth mayor from 1903-04. Mowbray died in Tulsa at age 62 in 1910.

TULSA HISTORICAL SOCIETY

Tulsa's newly expanded Frisco Depot at the railroad tracks and Boston Avenue, c.1908.

From that point forward, it's not too much to say that Tulsa was led by two bodies—both its official municipal government and Mowbray's unofficial congress of boosters and business leaders. The reality was that for the first half of Tulsa's life, city government operated merely in support of the far more powerful Commercial Club, later the Chamber of Commerce. As if to underscore the dynamics of this relationship, Reverend Mowbray moved directly from his position leading the Commercial Club into the position of leading city government, when he was elected as Tulsa's fifth mayor in 1903.

Before Mowbray became mayor, he and Hall led the effort to achieve the first strategic objective of the Commercial Club—overcoming Tulsa's geographical disadvantage of being isolated by the Arkansas River. Working as a two-man negotiating team,[15] they secured the realignment of three additional railroad lines through Tulsa—the Missouri-Kansas-Texas (the Katy) in 1902, and the Midland Valley Line in 1903. While in office, Mowbray continued the effort, and the Santa Fe rolled into town in 1905. The convergence of four rail lines and the remarkably fortuitous private development of the first vehicle bridge over the Arkansas in 1904 perfectly set the table for the discovery of the Glenn Pool oil reserve at the close of 1905.

Once the true potential of the Glenn Pool was fully realized, the development the boosters had dreamed of and labored for came so quickly that there seemed to be no word for it other than "magic." Over the course of fifteen electrifyingly short years, Tulsa would explode into a metropolis of nearly 100,000. In the era of boomtowns, Tulsa was the greatest of them all. It was the fastest-growing city in the world, boasting the greatest per-capita wealth. Tulsa was, indeed, the Magic City, capital of the Magic Empire awash in the magic of black gold. The pace of change was unimaginable, and it would take more than magic to manage it.

It would take a miracle.

REGULATING *the* GUSHER

I N HIS CENTENNIAL RETROSPECTIVE on the Glenn Pool, *Nearly Forgotten,* author Doug Hicks wrote that Glenn Pool oil would "create fortunes, cause havoc and joy, and trigger widespread growth as a new industry materialized… Honesty and corruption, generosity and greed, trust and distrust, wealth and poverty, good times and bad—all would arrive, reside, grow and emerge from the Glenn Pool."[1] And the fallout, both in its glory and in its repugnancy, would land squarely on the shoulders of Tulsa. ¶ Not unlike the lure of the infamous "gambling tents" that had fueled the disorder of Tulsa's cowtown years, it was the lure of excitement and dreams of wealth that fueled the chaos, danger,

4th City Hall (1906-1909)

City Hall

Northside of 2nd Street between Main and Boulder.
Completed one year after the Red Fork oil discovery, Tulsa's
first purpose-built City Hall building had a short life span.
Even with expansion that doubled its size, the city offices
couldn't keep pace with the rapid growth of Tulsa. The foul
odor of the fire department's stable also contributed to the
city commission's departure from the building.
Tulsa Historical Society

Birds-eye View of Glenn Pool Oil Field, near TULSA, Okla.

PUBLIC DOMAIN

OSAGE AM. NO. 9 INDI CURIO. CO.

HAND-COLORED.

dramatic sums of their personal incomes to Tulsa's legendary "stud notes." Discovered to be a proven formula for success, stud notes were private incentive packages that lured every industry from railroads to refineries into the city.

Not only were the members driven by a personal-profit motive that gave undeniable evidence to the philosophy that a rising tide lifts all boats, but there was also a vibrant and intoxicating spirit of audacity that emboldened every club member to think in terms of extra-governmental action. In their view, Tulsa *had to be* unstoppable. Where the process of government or the popular vote of the people failed to get a job done, Commercial Club members took action.

In addition to the stud notes that enticed the railroads to realign their course through Tulsa, it was also the private efforts of Commercial Club members that, in 1904, built the first badly

and adventure in the hunt for oil. It would, then, only stand to reason that the boomtowns fueled by oil could not help but reflect that same wildcatting ethos. Like the Glenn Pool, Tulsa's Commercial Club was running hot. Tulsa's business community— which was growing by the day—was like an uncapped gusher, squeezing every opportunity out of their good fortune. Capping the well, controlling the flow, and turning the mess into magic became a task so monumental that it had to be shared by both Tulsa's municipal government and the Commercial Club. Going well beyond the typical notions of civic responsibility and volunteerism, the Commercial Club's boosters pooled resources and pledged

needed vehicle bridge across the Arkansas River, after Tulsans voted down a bond to build it. Private club money was, in one way or another, involved in nearly every major industry that came to Tulsa before 1920. Not satisfied with merely wining and dining visiting capitalists, Tulsa boosters actually left town in search of anyone who had yet to hear the word "Tulsa." Traveling by rail in 1903, 1905, and 1907 on privately chartered trains, Tulsa boosters headed east to bring the story of their "Magic City" to the well-established parts of the country. Accompanied by the Commercial Club's own band—which was, by all accounts, exceptionally good—and local celebrities of national renown, like the reformed outlaw, Emmet Dalton, and an up-and-coming Will Rogers, they received tremendous attention and press—usually good, occasionally bad—virtually everywhere they went. In New York City, the governor and city officials gave Tulsa's boosters a 5th Avenue parade. In Washington, D.C., they received a standing ovation by a joint session of Congress and a party

THERE *was a* VIBRANT *and* INTOXICATING
SPIRIT *of* AUDACITY *that* EMBOLDENED
EVERY COMMERCIAL CLUB MEMBER.
in THEIR VIEW, TULSA
HAD to be UNSTOPPABLE.

arranged by President Roosevelt. In Chicago, they nearly started a riot and were run out of town in 1903, but, by 1907, they were received as honorees by the Chicago Board of Trade. By all accounts, these booster trips were remarkably impactful. Some of Tulsa's most prominent citizens, who invested millions in Tulsa's early development, and made millions more in return, came to town as a direct result of the booster trips.

While the Commercial Club was busy at work, Tulsa's municipal government struggled under the weight of the booming growth. Just keeping up with the most basic of city services was proving nearly impossible. Between 1900 and 1920, Tulsa experienced a 5,200-percent increase in population,[2] with the greatest peak of growth hitting between 1910 and 1912, when the city nearly doubled in size, from 18,182 to 31,525, in just two

Pictured in Springfield, Missouri, on March 14, 1905, the **Tulsa Boosters** toured the Eastern United States to promote the economic opportunities available in Tulsa, I.T. **Will Rogers**, age 27, can be seen in white shirt sleeves on the right side of picture. In addition to Tulsa's band, Rogers helped attract crowds and media. BERYL FORD COLLECTION

years.[3] Truly keeping up with growth on that scale was a practical impossibility. But even before the major population surges following the Glenn Pool discovery, Tulsa was still little more than a rural trading post in regard to basic services.

Although Tulsa had no paved street; no organized water, sewer, or electric services; and only a small handful of telephones, the club's first booster trip headed east in 1903 to sing the praises of a "progressive and modern city." Despite the optimism that pervaded the town, there was then, as now (and as always), the cynical ink slinger who busied himself throwing stones. Often the critic was Tulsa's own newspaper, the *Democrat*. In 1903, the paper bemoaned the condition of Tulsa by describing it as a "city in darkness and in mud! Without a lamp to cast one ray of light across the pathway of the benighted traveler as he gropes his way around mud holes and over dilapidated sidewalks. This is the condition that confronts the visitor to this fair city."[4]

The *Democrat's* dismal editorial of Tulsa came during Reverend Mowbray's administration. In fairness, Tulsa had only been a city for five years. And not only had it already tripled in size,

Pictured here in about 1910, citizen street pavers respond to a city law that required every able-bodied man to contribute labor to street work or pay a fine. BERYL FORD COLLECTION

TULSA BECAME *the* FIRST CITY *in the* NEW STATE *to* LEGALLY SEGREGATE—*an* ILL-FATED DECISION *that* STARTED *a* CHAIN *of* EVENTS *that* WOULD FOREVER MAR TULSA'S LEGACY *as a* HIGH-MINDED, MORAL, *and* PROGRESSIVE CITY.

but Mowbray's government was still working through the legal process of platting, appraising, selling, and taxing land. There was plenty of public support for improvements, and the city council was trying to respond to the will of the people. But up until Oklahoma's statehood, Tulsa still faced legal obstacles connected to being within the borders of Indian Territory. Municipalities could not yet incur debt, and thus they had no clear legal option[5] for passing city bond issues.[6] Tulsa's leadership did, however, come up with a few unique solutions.

To both fund street paving and silence the critics, a 1906 ordinance was passed requiring every man in Tulsa between eighteen and forty-five to either contribute a full day's labor to the effort of street paving once a year until the task was done, or pay a special onetime, three-dollar street tax. Money arrived faster than conscripted laborers, and real progress started to be made.[7]

WITH THE notable exception of Tulsa's notoriously bad water, the continuing partnership between city government and the Commercial Club solved crisis after crisis, and eventually, publicly and privately owned utility services, public transportation, and especially schools, showed dramatic improvements everywhere—except for the systemically underserved and neglected Greenwood District. Greenwood had been established in 1905 as a self-segregated development with great hope and promise for optimistic African Americans in search of opportunity in the Magic City. However, the following year, the Republican-led Oklahoma Territory, which had been considered a safe haven by many black pioneers, entered statehood with a Democratic majority whose first official legislative action (Senate Bill One) was the institution of Jim Crow laws. Under the Democratic administration of Tulsa's tenth mayor, W.E. Rohde, Tulsa followed suit in 1908. Upon rewriting

Entrepreneurialism thrived in Tulsa's Greenwood District for more than 50 years. African American business owners, clergy, and educators overcame unimaginable obstacles to create a cultural and economic phenomenon that, sadly, remains overshadowed by the tragedy of the Tulsa Race Riot. *Above left:* Looking north on Greenwood from Archer, c.1921. *Above Right*: Lennie and Clark Holderness standing in front of the first cleaning business in Greenwood, 1925. Tulsa Historical Society

the city charter to adapt to Oklahoma's new constitution, Tulsa became the first city in the new state to legally segregate—an ill-fated decision that started a chain of events that would forever mar Tulsa's legacy as a high-minded, moral, and progressive city.

The more oil wealth that rolled into Tulsa, the more it became clear that systemic bigotry wasn't the only issue that chronically plagued the city. The sensational highs from oil fortunes that could be made nearly overnight—often by men unprepared emotionally to deal with it—brought a culture of vice the likes of which Tulsa had never seen, even in its wild years. Tulsa's original crop of pioneers who had fought so hard to establish a moral foundation for the wild little cowtown had become "old-timers." Having availed himself of the unique honor of preaching his own funeral, Reverend Mowbray passed away in 1910. Colonel Calkins died the following year, and J.M. Hall, nearing retirement age and with weakening health, began withdrawing from his business interests in 1912. No doubt discouraged by the open depravity of the city he'd guided into greatness, Hall took a back seat in the Commercial Club and, instead,

focused considerable attention on the institution he ultimately embraced as his legacy—The University of Tulsa.

The moral idealism of the old guard was becoming increasingly replaced by an ethos of leniency that quietly acknowledged the reality that vice was good for business. Rumors of Tulsa's prostitution, gambling, and bootlegged liquor lured big spenders from across the region like moths to a flame. The Oil Capital's seedy underside lived up to the rumors, as did the violence and victimization that inevitably came with it. Despite all the progress that had been made since the explosion at the Archer Store, brawls and murders were once again common occurrences on Tulsa's now-paved streets. With what had become an undeniable red-light district along 1st Street, Tulsa's dark side began to change the public's view of itself. And once the passions of the constituency were aroused, the situation became "intolerable" to the public façade of every politician. Although more in word than deed, cleaning up the city became the top issue for both parties, starting with the election of 1910.

In what was probably his last major attempt at citywide moral guidance, J.M. Hall chaired a

nonpartisan campaign initiative that year, with the hopes of electing a mayor who had the determination to do what was necessary to cleanse the city. Hall's group nominated H.O. McClure, who ran as an independent. McClure lost to the Democrat, Loyal J. Martin, but as it turned out, Martin became a far stronger crusader against vice than McClure could ever have been.

Martin started his administration by firing any officials he considered compromised, and replacing them with hard-nosed men of action like Charles W. Conneely, whom he appointed the chief of police. Not only did Martin *not* look the other way, but he personally joined Conneely on police raids that systematically hit every known gambling house, brothel, and speakeasy in town.[8] Martin and Conneely met their objective of cleaning up Tulsa, but only to the extent that they pushed Tulsa's red-light district outside the city limits, where business flourished and, according to the *Tulsa Daily World*, "put to shame the rotten days of ancient Rome."[9] As a reward for his stalwart pursuit of public decency and fidelity to his campaign promises, Martin was voted out in 1912 and was said to have left office friendless.[10]

In a backlash against Martin's crusading, F.M. Wooden became Tulsa's twelfth mayor. Wooden, another kind of Democrat entirely, quickly developed a well-deserved reputation for leniency that ultimately served him no better than it did the city. Wooden installed

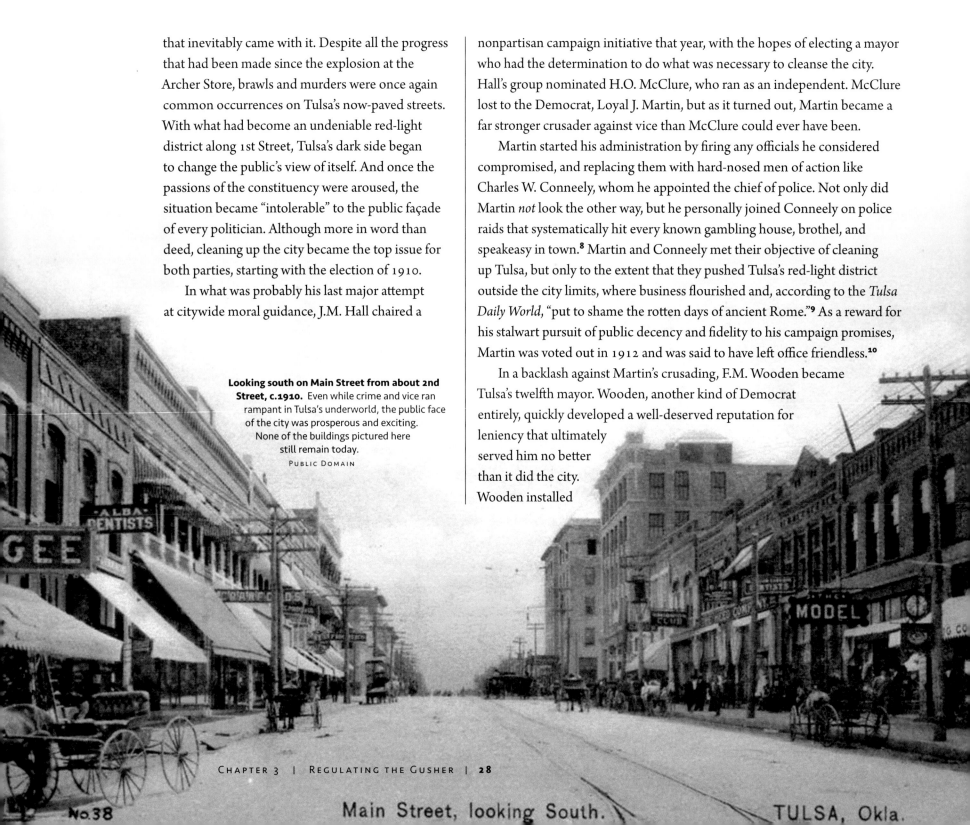

Looking south on Main Street from about 2nd Street, c.1910. Even while crime and vice ran rampant in Tulsa's underworld, the public face of the city was prosperous and exciting. None of the buildings pictured here still remain today.
PUBLIC DOMAIN

ALBA DENTISTS
GEE

MODEL

No.38

Main Street, looking South.

TULSA, Okla.

LOYAL J. MARTIN
11th MAYOR of TULSA [1910-1912]

KNOWN AS "THE CRUSADING MAYOR," Loyal J. Martin spent his life doing more than talking about community justice. He walked the walk— even when it included personally accompanying the police department on vice raids during his term as Tulsa's eleventh mayor. His vice-busting was so successful that it cost him his bid for re-election.

Born in Crawford County, Ohio, in 1863, Martin attended Knox College in Illinois before graduating from the University of Michigan in 1889. Prior to Tulsa, he had served South Dakota's Miner County as its county attorney and as a state senator. But more than fighting against Tulsa's dark side of vice, Martin, having become a district judge after his term as mayor, was driven by his profound hunger for justice to impose himself as a leader in urging Tulsa to face the realities and consequences of the 1921 Race Riot.

As reported in *The Nation* magazine, Martin, identified as the chairman of the "emergency committee," famously said: "Tulsa can only redeem herself from the country-wide shame and humiliation into which she is today plunged by complete restitution and rehabilitation of the destroyed black belt. The rest of the United States must know that the real citizenship of Tulsa weeps at this unspeakable crime and will make good the damage, so far as it can be done, to the last penny."

PUBLIC DOMAIN

his own police chief, Foster N. Burns,[11] and, under his administration, vice, violence, and crime infected Tulsa worse than before. The scourge continued unabated until tragedy struck on July 23, 1914, when two United States deputy marshals were killed by a former Tulsa police chief-turned-bootlegger named William Barber.[12]

The incident occurred outside the front door of Barber's home as one of the marshals attempted to force entry to conduct a warrantless liquor raid. Barber shot both marshals at close range with a double-barrel shotgun. Given the lack of a warrant, Barber might have had a good argument for self-defense, had he not then reloaded and shot them again as they lay dying.[13] The next day, more than five thousand outraged citizens crowded in protest at the intersection of 4th & Main.

Declaring Tulsa to be utterly lawless, they officially petitioned the governor of the State of Oklahoma for help. Eventually, a grand jury was convened, and Mayor Wooden, Chief Burns,[14] and other officials were found guilty of taking bribes from the worst elements of Tulsa's underworld. Wooden was removed from office in 1916, becoming the only mayor in Tulsa's history to be impeached.[15]

While the reality of Tulsa's underworld would, for generations, continue to foster salacious tales worthy of the trashiest true-crime magazines, vice would never again enjoy free rein corrupting even the highest offices of the city.

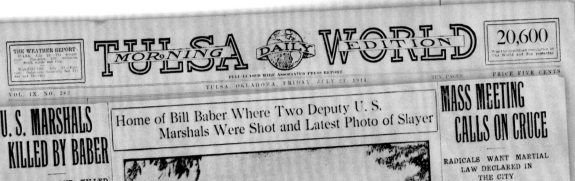

Following Wooden's impeachment, Tulsa elected John Simmons to be the city's thirteenth mayor. A charter member of the Commercial Club (which had, on October 20, 1915, incorporated as the Tulsa Chamber of Commerce), Simmons was the first Republican[16] to hold the office since Colonel Calkins, eighteen years earlier. In the run-up to his election, Simmons boldly proclaimed, "The city needs a house cleaning, officially speaking. And one of the first acts of the Republican administration after taking office will be to uncover all crookedness and graft that has been reported to be going on at city hall."[17] He was right about the need for a good housecleaning. To that end, his election wasn't merely a product of the popular vote, but also a sign that the powerful Chamber of Commerce was once again flexing its muscles.

According to official Chamber notes,[18] the clarion call for reform had come in the summer of 1915, when a representative of the Harrison Machine Works of Belleville, Illinois, flatly told the chamber that his company wanted to move to Tulsa, but once their investigations had revealed how bad vice in the city was, he "could not recommend the transfer of his associates as long as these conditions prevailed."[19]

The Chamber got the message and, on August 23, 1915, made an internal resolution to "clean up gambling and illegal selling of liquor in Tulsa."[20] The same promise had been publicly made by every politician for the last ten years. But when the Chamber acted behind closed doors, things happened quickly. The indictments against Mayor Wooden's administration were filed less than four months later. When Simmons, whom the Chamber supported, won the election the following spring, he and his fellow Republican aldermen swept the ticket by the greatest margins ever seen in Tulsa politics.[21]

During the long preoccupation with vice, many municipal projects had been neglected. In retrospect, the greatest problem at the time was the ongoing disregard of infrastructure and services within the

Police Chief Herman Newblock (*first row, white hat*), an experienced lawman and future mayor, stands with members of the **1912 Tulsa Police Department**. Newblock's tenure as chief was noted for what a history of the Tulsa Police Department termed a "lasting innovation"—assigning police officers to direct traffic at downtown's busiest intersections—a sign of a growing city. First sites for the innovation, which lasted for fifty years, were 2nd & Main, and 3rd & Main. With the police department subject to change with each election cycle at that time, Chief Newblock became ex-Chief Newblock following the April 1912 city election. Beryl Ford Collection

BOTH POLITICAL PARTIES, *the* COMMERCIAL CLUB, EVEN *the* NEWSPAPERS, SHARED *a* COMMON VIEW *that* PRESTIGIOUS PUBLIC BUILDINGS *were* PREREQUISITE ELEMENTS, NECESSARY *to* SHOW *the* OUTSIDE WORLD THAT TULSA *was a* PROGRESSIVE *and* COSMOPOLITAN ISLAND *of* GRANDEUR *and* SOPHISTICATION.

Greenwood District. While those issues would remain largely unanswered, to the peril of Tulsa's future, the agenda item topping the Chamber's list for Mayor Simmons would be of equal benefit to all of Tulsa—finally solving the chronic problem of Tulsa's water supply. At the time of his election, the situation was so bad that it was not uncommon for guests and residents to find rings of Arkansas River mud lining sinks and basins. Despite the grand, world-class architecture on the exterior of Tulsa's pre-1925 buildings, many of them relied on their own water wells dug deep below their basements, because city water was deemed undrinkable.

The second issue of neglect on Simmons's list was, all things considered, a rather surprising one. By the time Simmons was elected, Tulsa had enjoyed a fifteen-year unbroken building boom. Commercial construction was rising as fast as labor and materials would allow. Residential construction could not come close to keeping pace with demand. As one would expect, the Commercial Club had driven hard to see that Tulsa had public buildings in keeping with the city's image of sophistication and power. The first opera house opened in 1906. Tulsa County had raised a beautiful neoclassical courthouse in 1913. After much effort, Convention Hall had come together in 1914. The following year, a YMCA opened. The new pride of the city, the Andrew Carnegie City Library, came in the summer of 1916, and, already under construction, a new federal building and post office was slated to open in 1917. Yet, in the Chamber's rush to keep Tulsa growing and functioning, and throughout the city's fight against vice and mismanagement, neither institution   time to find a place they could call home.

Tulsa's City Commission.
A hurricane was responsible for the City Commission form of government that led Tulsa before and after the Municipal Building served as Tulsa's city hall. The 1900 hurricane that killed 6,000 citizens of Galveston, Texas, prompted that Gulf Coast city's leaders to propose an organization with at-large elected officials assuming both legislative and administrative (as in head of city departments) roles. The idea spread rapidly, and from 1907 to 1920, with about 500 cities signing on. Tulsa was an early adopter when voters approved it on July 3, 1908. Oklahoma Governor Charles N. Haskell formally approved its installation on January 5, 1909. That system—with a mayor, four commissioners and a city auditor elected for two-year terms—stayed in effect until citizens approved a new city charter in 1989.

BERYL FORD COLLECTION

"*With the* PURCHASE *of a* SITE
at the INTERSECTION *of* FOURTH *and* CINCINNATI *for the* ERECTION *of a*
MUNICIPAL BUILDING, MAYOR JOHN H. SIMMONS *and the*
BOARD *of* CITY COMMISSIONERS *have* PLACED *the* KEYSTONE *into*
a TEMPLE *of* ACHIEVEMENT *which* THEY HOPE WILL STAND FOREVER
as a MONUMENT *to* THEIR ADMINISTRATION."

FROM PAGE FIFTY-SEVEN

A TEMPLE *of* ACHIEVEMENT

M V N I C I P A L   B V I L D I N G

The MISSING PIECE

BUILDING A BEAUTIFUL HOME for city government was not Mayor Simmons's idea. It was merely another item on a long list of problems left up to his administration to solve. The problem of an adequate city hall was not a consequence of Tulsa having never built one. Rather, like everything else about Tulsa following the Glenn Pool discovery, Tulsa's first city hall was outgrown as quickly as it opened, and it had to be abandoned less than five years after it was erected. The want, need, and struggle for a suitable replacement would haunt Tulsa's next eight administrations. Despite a great deal of talk and some over-the-top machinations, no mayor had yet managed to solve the problem.

4TH CITY HALL (1909-1910)
Egan Building

West side of Main between 1st and 2nd Streets. Officing above the first location of Tulsa's famous Vandevers store, Mayor John O. Mitchell failed to rid the city of the red light district despite being less than a block away.

5TH CITY HALL (1910-1912)
Shutts Building

East side of Boston between 1st and 2nd Streets. Loyal J. Martin personally led vice raids during his tenure in the Shutts Building. The building included a shooting range in the basement.

6TH CITY HALL (1912-1919)
Reeder Building

Northeast corner of 2nd & Boston. Despite calls for a "real" city hall, the issue was put to temporary rest after the city commission signed an initial two-year lease on the Reeder Building. Mayor Wooden led the infamous Vice Trust from his office in the Reeder Building.

PARISIAN CLEANERS & DYERS
HATTERS & TAILORS Phone 697

1ST CITY HALL (1836–1861)
Council Oak Tree

18th & Cheyenne. Though it has never been called one of Tulsa's "city halls," the Council Oak Tree, where the first council fire was built at the end of the Trail of Tears, marked the beginning of local government in the area.

OKLAHOMA HISTORICAL SOCIETY

2ND CITY HALL (1882–1897)
Hall & Co. Store

Northwest corner of 1st & Main. The first official "seat" of government was the front porch of Tulsa pioneer J.M. Hall's store. What started as dreams and schemes quickly evolved into a real agenda for civic growth.

BERYL FORD COLLECTION

Looking back on the mind-set of Tulsa's early leadership, a city hall was an unlikely piece to be left out of the development puzzle. Both political parties, the Commercial Club, even the newspapers, shared a common view that prestigious public buildings were prerequisite elements, necessary to show the outside world that Tulsa was a progressive and cosmopolitan island of grandeur and sophistication, standing in stark contrast to its location within a land still thought by most outsiders to be the Wild West teeming with outlaws and Indian raiding parties. But with all the pots that were kept at a rapid boil by economic growth and the corruption that accompanied it, getting around to building a city hall worthy of a Magic City uncharacteristically fell by the wayside.

Until Simmons's election, the housing of Tulsa's leadership had been a nearly comical drama, slowly playing itself out for some thirty-five years. Going back to the days before Tulsa was a city in need of a city hall, the front porch of the Hall & Company store was where future city fathers gathered to share stories, gossip, make plans, and dream up wild schemes about how their little Indian trading post

could someday hit the big time. By 1893, the men had moved to significantly better accommodations on the second floor of the new sandstone Lynch Building, located on the southeast corner of 2nd & Main. That would likely have been the first meeting place of Tulsa's official city government, had the Great Fire of 1897 not nearly destroyed it just five weeks before Tulsa got her charter. Although severely damaged, the Lynch Building was the only structure on the block to have survived. One other unlikely but fortuitous survivor of the fire was the safe from Tulsa's only bank, which had also originally operated out of the Hall & Company store. So, along with the money, Tulsa's first city council returned to the Hall Store, where the bank and the city operated in an official capacity until repairs were completed on the Lynch Building.

Plans to construct Tulsa's first proper city hall were announced in March of 1905.[1] The building got an interesting mention on the front page of the very first issue of the *Tulsa Daily World*, forerunner of the *Tulsa World*. Just below the fold on page 1, volume 1, number 1, on September 14, 1905, can be found a headline reading: "City Hall Foundation Completed." The content of the short article is an amusing reminder that some things about government never change: It seems the project was behind schedule and experiencing funding issues.[2]

Erected on the northeast corner of 2nd & Boulder, the first city hall was completed and began occupancy on January 26, 1906.[3] Today, the Tulsa Fire Department's centennial memorial—"Courage and Compassion for 100 Years," by sculptor Denise Rinkovsky—stands just a little to the west of the site.

3RD CITY HALL (1897-1906)

Lynch Building

Southeast corner of 1st & Main. Five weeks before Tulsa received its charter, the Lynch Building was severely damaged by fire. After repairs, the second floor housed the first official city offices.

4TH CITY HALL (1906-1909)

City Hall

North side of 2nd between Main and Boulder. Originally an all-purpose city building, the fire department became its sole occupant due to the aroma generated by their horses housed on the ground floor.

Although the cornice marker bore the title "CITY HALL," it was actually a mixed-use building, with city offices and the police court upstairs, and the fire department—including stables for its horses—at street level. The basement was constructed with concrete walls and iron bars to serve as the city jail.[4] Although the building housed all the city's office needs, it is only remembered today for its role as Tulsa's first fire department. This is likely because the smell of the department's horses drove off the other city offices in fairly short order.

By June of that same year, Mayor John O. Mitchell, Tulsa's ninth mayor, was already ordering plans for an addition to the building that would more than double both the city's office space and, importantly, the jail capacity.[5] But even that expansion did little to satisfy the need for the booming city. In 1908, Mayor Rohde's administration, working in concert with the Commercial Club, put forth its solution to the city hall problem by combining a stylish new city hall with the city's other great need, a convention hall. In one of the Commercial Club's rare upsets, the voters said no.[6] The Commercial Club continued to push hard for the combined hall plan. It wasn't until January 21, 1913, that voters passed a bond to build Convention Hall, which is known today as the venerable Brady Theater. By then, however, a city hall inclusion had been dropped from the plan.

With the failure of Mayor Rohde's 1908 bond, Tulsa's city hall became an orphan destined to spend almost a decade sojourning through a series of disjoined professional spaces or squeezed into cramped and inadequate city buildings. In 1909, City Hall found itself on the second floor of Egan Building at 111 South

"Courage and Compassion for 100 Years." In 2007, the location of Tulsa's first city hall building, which was also Tulsa's first fire department, was memorialized by the Tulsa Fire Department as a part of their first centennial celebration with the dedication of an eight-foot bronze sculpture by Denise Rinkovsky. DOUGLAS MILLER

Main Street above the Beane-Vandever Dry Goods Company,[7] predecessor of Tulsa's famous Vandevers Department Store. In October 1910, it moved to the third floor of the Shutts Building, a modest three-story commercial space adjacent to the Central National Bank on the east side of Boston between 1st and 2nd Streets. The Shutts Building was linked to the bank, so visitors entered city hall through the bank's lobby. The city hoped the bank would also provide elevator service, but when they declined, City Hall made its third move in as many years, this time across the street to the third and fourth floors of the Reeder Building, located on the

northeast corner of 2nd & Boston.[8] The recipient of City Hall's rent check then became Dr. C.L. Reeder, who was both a long-serving member of the Commercial Club as well as Tulsa's seventh mayor, the first mayor to confront the aftermath of the Glenn Pool discovery.

The move into the Reeder Building occurred in June 1912, just after the transition between Mayors Martin and Wooden. Not only is Mayor Wooden remembered for being the only Tulsa mayor to have been impeached, but, ironically, he was also the first Tulsa mayor to win re-election. Thus, the confusion, corruption, and longevity of the Wooden years contributed greatly to what turned into a very long and arduous stay in the Reeder Building. Whether writing about a city commissioner having to leap for his life from a runaway elevator, to bemoaning overcrowding and suffering through interior deluges, newspapermen of the day were never lacking for space fillers about the intolerable conditions in the Reeder Building. Yet the city would be doomed to maintain its offices there, in one form or another, for the next seven years.

As City Hall continued to expand to meet the insatiable needs of the booming city, the individual departments that were lucky enough to outgrow the Reeder Building found space wherever they could. The first to

DR. C.L. REEDER
7th MAYOR *of* TULSA [1905-1906]

In addition to being a skilled physician, Dr. Reeder was one of the hardest-working developers of early Tulsa. He contributed much of his own time, money, and energy to establishing many of the fundamental services needed by a growing city, including safe natural gas services, clean water, and fire protection. Working with Dr. Fred S. Clinton, Dr. Reeder also played a vital role in establishing Tulsa's first hospital.

BERYL FORD COLLECTION

7TH CITY HALL (1912-1919)

Reeder Building

Northeast corner of 2nd & Boston. A move across the street lent a modicum of relative permanence as an initial two-year lease was extended until a "permanent" Municipal Building could be built.

8TH CITY HALL (1919-1969)

Municipal Building

Southeast corner of 4th & Cincinnati. At last a home, an impressive structure for a growing city—that is until it became too small, too old, too much to maintain. Regardless, it served as Tulsa's city hall for 50 years.

NOT ONLY *is* MAYOR WOODEN REMEMBERED *for* BEING *the* ONLY TULSA MAYOR *to have been* IMPEACHED, *but,* IRONICALLY, HE *was* ALSO *the* FIRST TULSA MAYOR *to* WIN RE-ELECTION.

go were the police and fire administrations. In 1913, the city acquired an old livery stable just east of Boulder on the north side of 2nd Street and converted it into a conjoined office for both departments, along with an expanded city jail in the basement *(see page 45)*.[9]

Either despite or because of Wooden's leniency toward vice, the expanded jail was already overcrowded and in a deplorable condition by the end of 1914. Described by a *Morning Tulsa Daily World* editorial as a "Bastille unfit for human habitation,"[10] the jail was bad enough to have become a liability, "condemned by every representative of prison conditions that has ever visited the city."[11] In addition to the fear of lawsuits by their own inmates, city commissioners had long been concerned by the $300-per-month price tag for housing the city offices in the Reeder Building (equivalent to about $7,100 per month in 2017 dollars). While inexpensive by today's standards, in a time when new construction, even in a boomtown, was dramatically less expensive than today, the continued leasing option was rightly viewed as a significant waste of the taxpayers' money.

The pressing problems regarding inadequate city facilities, combined with the mounting trials and abject distrust of Wooden's administration, demanded movement on the question of a city hall. In February 1915, Mayor Wooden finally put forth his plan to address both the woes of City Hall and the city jail. For as long as the city commission had waited for Wooden's plan, it turned out to be wholly uninspiring.

IN ADDITION to administrative malfeasance, bribery, graft, and corruption, one more accusation could apparently be leveled against Mayor Wooden: He was cheap. His "permanent solution" for Tulsa's city hall was to simply remodel and expand the already overcrowded and troublesome police and fire station on 2nd Street. Wooden intended to address the overcrowding by adding a second story to house all the city offices that were currently

FRANK M. WOODEN

12*th* MAYOR *of* TULSA [1912-1916]

FRANK WOODEN CAME TO TULSA from Houston in 1906 as a wholesaler of animal hides but quickly found his way onto the public payroll. Running as a Democrat in 1910, he won his first elected position as Tulsa's commissioner of finance and revenue in the administration of Mayor Loyal J. Martin. As a known supporter of "open-town" policies regarding Tulsa's prohibition laws, Wooden's star rose quickly and, after only two years in politics, he soundly defeated Mayor Martin—a fellow Democrat but aggressive vice-buster. Wooden enjoyed political popularity until his open-town policies proved to be too open. By his second term in office, Tulsa had entered a dark period of crime, corruption, and violence. The state stepped in and Wooden was removed from office before the end of his term.

His ultimate conviction for corruption did nothing to stop his political successes. After two brief years spent in the private sector while unsuccessfully fighting the charges against him, Wooden was, in 1918, elected as commissioner for the first district of Tulsa County. In the aftermath of the 1921 Tulsa Race Riots, he made a shocking bid for a third term as Tulsa mayor with an ironic promise to clean up the town. Although beaten in the primary by Herman Newblock, Wooden was seemingly never truly defeated. Later that same year, 1922, he was re-elected as county commissioner and continued to find various state and county political appointments for the rest of his long career in Democratic politics.

PUBLIC DOMAIN

9TH CITY HALL (1969-2007)

City Hall Tower

200 Civic Center. Despite four decades of longing for a majestic, wholly modernistic civic center, what was to be the ultimate city hall only survived 38 years before being abandoned.

CITY OF TULSA

10TH CITY HALL (2007-)

One Technology Center

Northwest corner of 2nd & Cincinnati. With the promise to save and make the city money by buying a building, using needed space, and leasing the rest, City Hall moved back into a commercial office space.

DOUGLAS MILLER

occupying two floors in the Reeder Building. It was a plan doomed from the start, and such was pointed out by someone who actually worked in the existing 2nd Street building: Tulsa's first, still-serving, and revered fire chief, R.C. Alder.

Within three weeks of Wooden's announcement, Chief Alder had an alternate plan in front of the commission, which called for clearing the 2nd Street lot and raising a new "three-story building with every convenience of a modern municipal building."[12] He argued that new construction made more economic sense than "adding a story to the present building thus leaving much to be desired."[13] As uninspiring as Wooden's plan was, however, it did have one significant advantage: With an estimated cost of only $20,000, it could be funded by a simple bank loan, thus sidestepping the need to ask voters to pass a bond. Alder's plan, exceptionally modest as it was, would require no less than $60,000—just enough to necessitate a vote of the people.[14]

Albeit with great trepidation, the commission accepted Wooden's plan, pending approval from engineers. Their decision was not unanimous, and those commissioners who sided with Alder were supported by area businessmen who, although happy to see any improvement in the city jail, had strongly supported Alder's plan, assuming that even a modest new city hall would have a better impact on their property values.[15] On April 17, 1915, the *Morning Tulsa Daily World* editorialized the sentiments of most of those

Rolla Alder, Tulsa's first fire chief.
Alder came to Tulsa in March 1900 to establish himself as a harness and saddlemaker. He volunteered to lead the fire brigade, serving for free until he was hired as the first full-time chief in 1905. Alder served with the Tulsa Fire Department until his retirement in 1922. He passed away in 1967.
BERYL FORD COLLECTION

involved: "Many would prefer, from reasons of civic pride, to see a new city hall built that would be in harmony with the city's progress and adequate for future needs; but it is urged that economic reasons make it necessary to be content with what is available, rather than what is desirable."[16]

In the end, however, the debate was rendered moot, after a thorough examination of the site

TULSA RETAINS REPUTATION OF DOING THINGS

Splendid Vote Polled and Townbuilders Overcome Disgruntled Element.

SEWERS GIVEN THE BIGGEST MAJORITY

Heaviest Vote Ever Cast at Bond Election; Means a Greater City.

THE VOTE.

	Yes.	No.	Maj.
City Hall	830	617	213
Sewers	920	531	389
Boulevards and parks	771	674	97

TULSA goes forward! All three bond issues won out in yesterday's election by majorities of 97 for the park and boulevard issue, 213 for the city hall and 389 for sewers.

A total of 1,451 votes were cast. It was the largest vote ever recorded at a strictly bond election in this city. Previous bond issues voted here have received total votes ranging from one-third to one-tenth of the total vote cast yesterday, and all of them have been approved by eminent attorneys and found ready markets.

No Question as to Legality.

There is no question as to the legality of yesterday's election. A few persons, who contended that the total vote must amount to 50 per cent of the vote cast in the last preceeding general election, were thinking of the law that applies to initiated bills, and not municipal bond elections. The city attorney's office has been in communication with the attorney general's office for the past two weeks and private messages received show positively that it was a legal election from every standpoint and point to the early approval of all the bonds by the attorney general of the state.

The large vote is credited to the bitter fight waged against the bonds, largely on political grounds and because of personal animosity against the city administration. But the broad-minded voters of the town went to the polls and voted for the good of

(Continued on Page Two.)

Fortunately, voting in Tulsa has evolved since 1915.

Tulsa's early voting system was significantly lacking in equality and fairness. Out of a population of more than 30,000 residents, only 1,451 individuals cast ballots in the June 19, 1915, bond election that approved the initial funding for the Municipal Building. And *that* was considered a large turnout. Although on the cusp of winning suffrage, Women could not yet vote. Also turned away were men deemed non-taxpayers or those who did not qualify based on locally determined voting statutes. To quote the *Morning Tulsa Daily World's* report assuring the "validity" of the vote's outcome: **"Usual precautions were taken in every instance to see that each man who voted was a qualified elector and a taxpayer, according to the statues. Scores of men who went to the polls were denied a vote because they did not come up to the legal qualifications. It is a notable fact that in the precinct where reside practically all of the Negro voters of the city a total of only 45 votes were cast."**

determined that the state of the existing building was so questionable that even securing financing for a renovation was unlikely. In May 1915, both Wooden's remodeling plan and Alder's plan for a new building were abandoned. The most practical decision was to select a new location and ask the people for a $100,000 bond to build a proper city hall. The existing building on 2nd Street should then be remodeled, the commission decided, and given exclusively to either the police or the fire department. This decision started a contest between the police commissioner, Thomas J. Quinn, and Chief Alder for control of the location. In Commissioner Quinn's warning to the public regarding the severity of overcrowding at the jail, he said the situation was so dire that they might soon be forced to racially integrate prisoners.[17]

Fearing critics who argued that an opulent city hall was a self-serving and unwarranted indulgence by the city's leadership, the commission packaged the city hall bond with two other bonds, one practical and one popular. The official request to the citizens of Tulsa was for $100,000 for sewer extensions, $100,000 for parks and boulevards, and $125,000 for a new municipal hall "commensurate with the city."[18] Before going to the vote of the people, however, it was customary for significant financial matters to be debated behind closed doors by an assembly of Commercial Club members that included the "heaviest taxpayers" in the city. Out of the three bonds, word that a new and prestigious city hall would finally become a reality garnered the most enthusiasm, especially from Paul M. Gallaway, presiding member of the committee and manager of the Public Service Corporation.

"A Bastille unfit for human habitation." After years of complaints and real concerns about litigation and the outbreak of various epidemics, the Oklahoma Commissioner of Charities and Corrections condemned Tulsa's notorious City Jail in 1916. The City of Tulsa signed its first contract with Tulsa County to house inmates until a new jail could be constructed. To avoid the complications of transferring the existing prisoners, on moving day, Tulsa's chief of police surprised all but one of his inmates with a one-time "get out of jail free" card. Beryl Ford Collection

MAYOR PRO TEM O.D. HUNT SPLASHED AROUND *the* ROOM, DECRYING THOSE WHO *had* VOTED AGAINST *the* BOND: *"And they say we don't need a city hall!"*

"If we are to have a high school costing $300,000," Gallaway proclaimed, "our city hall should not cost a cent less."[19]

The bonds met with unanimous approval from the committee.[20] And although not entirely free of opposition, the people of Tulsa liked the city's plans as well. Two weeks later, on Friday, June 18, 1915, voters passed all three with ease.[21] A surprisingly complicated road still lay ahead, but the City of Tulsa's long quest for a permanent address had finally become a tangible reality.

On the following Tuesday, the cantankerous Reeder Building reacted to the now-inevitable news of its pending replacement, by punishing the city commissioners for plotting against it. In an act of passive-aggressive defiance,

the building inundated the first meeting of the commission following the vote with a half-inch of runoff from heavy spring rains. With water pouring through fissures in the ceiling of the fourth-floor auditorium, city officials hurried through their business with pants rolled up and feet perched on the rungs of their chairs. According to the *Morning Tulsa Daily World*, Mayor Pro Tem O.D. Hunt splashed around the room, decrying those who had voted against the bond: "And they say we don't need a city hall!"[22]

CLEANING HOUSE

DESPITE THE PASSAGE OF the city hall bond, it seemed the Reeder Building would have the last laugh after all. The many complications of civic development within the Magic Empire, along with Mayor Wooden's problems with vice and corruption, would conspire to keep Tulsa's government trapped in the Reeder's ramshackle clutches for another three long years. ¶ In the passage of a bond election, the people agreed to pay interest on bonds sold by the city. Under Oklahoma law, however, the legality of the transaction had to be approved by the state's attorney general both before and after the sale of the bonds. Tulsa's great enthusiasm for a new city hall was

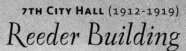

7284.   Reader Building, Tulsa, Okla.

7TH CITY HALL (1912-1919)
Reeder Building

Northeast corner of 2nd & Boston. Mayor Wooden's across-the-street move that made the Reeder Building Tulsa's City Hall in 1912 was prompted by access to an elevator. And that's about all the city got out of the move—and even that, not reliably. What started as a two-year lease until a proper city hall could be built labored on for seven years of misery for city operations.

PUBLIC DOMAIN

Oklahoma State Capitol, 1916. Delays in construction of the State Capitol, and a backup of municipal bond issues requiring the state Attorney General's approval, delayed Tulsa's City Hall.
WESLEY WINFORD, COURTESY OF THE OKLAHOMA HISTORICAL SOCIETY [2012.201.B0163B.0269]

S. Prince Freeling, Oklahoma Attorney General.
Gov. Robert L. Williams pledged that his state attorney general would personally conduct the investigations into any wrongdoing discovered in Tulsa by a grand jury empaneled under District Judge Conn Linn. That investigation gained national attention with the exposure of Tulsa's "Vice Trust."
EDWARD M. BOX COLLECTION, COURTESY OF THE OKLAHOMA HISTORICAL SOCIETY [1996.010]

Conn Linn, District Judge.
Prompted by law and order calls after two lawmen were shot by a former police chief, Judge Conn Linn empaneled the grand jury that, among other things, discovered "pay-for-play" involving city and county officials, and Tulsa's underworld.
PUBLIC DOMAIN

dampened by what would ultimately become a combined fourteen-month backlog at the desk of Oklahoma's newly elected attorney general, S.P. Freeling. In another twist of irony, the first of two chief causes for the delay was the state government's own woes with its working conditions. At the time when Tulsa submitted the bonds for its city hall, Oklahoma's new state capitol building had yet to be completed. Just like Tulsa's city offices, Oklahoma's state offices were orphans, working from rented rooms in the Lee-Huckins Hotel and various other offices scattered around Oklahoma City.

The second significant factor that delayed Freeling's approval of the bond was the attorney general's workload. Oklahoma was booming with oil wealth, and the AG's office was inundated with bonds from virtually every city and county that had an oil well. But from the fall of 1915 through the spring of 1916, Attorney General Freeling's schedule was further complicated by other matters in Tulsa far more pressing than reviewing and approving bonds. By no coincidence, Mayor Wooden also found himself with little interest in pushing for a city hall that, he'd come to realize, he would never occupy himself. And at the end of 1915, Wooden and his administration had bigger problems to deal with—problems that, unlike the city hall bond, attracted the immediate and full attention of Attorney General Freeling.

On October 31, 1915, a morally incensed District Judge Conn Linn empaneled the grand jury for which Tulsa's law-and-order community had advocated since the shootings of the two U.S. marshals in the summer of

"It is CONFIDENTLY EXPECTED *that* BEFORE *the* INQUISITORIAL BODY CONCLUDES *its* PROBE, TULSA COUNTY *will have* UNDERGONE *the* GREATEST UPHEAVAL *in its* HISTORY." *The ensuing legal drama was everything it was predicted to be.*

1914—and that the Chamber of Commerce had voted to support in the summer of 1915. With the sincere intention of putting a stop to the rampant vice that infected Tulsa and its surroundings, Judge Linn openly accused Tulsa's city and county leadership of being "engaged in the most flagrant, open, public, and notorious violation of the prohibitory and gambling laws of the state."[1] In this bold accusation, he leveled charges of corruption, collusion, and malfeasance against every single official within the borders of Tulsa County. Despite the audacity and the scope of his charges, Judge Linn was able to move aggressively and with confidence, because, prior to agreeing to call the grand jury, he had secured a personal guarantee from Oklahoma Governor Robert L. Williams that Attorney General Freeling would come to Tulsa personally to conduct all necessary investigations and prosecutions. Once Governor Williams agreed and Judge Linn announced his intentions, newspapers across the region reported: "It is confidently expected that before the inquisitorial body concludes its probe, Tulsa County will have undergone the greatest upheaval in its history."[2] The ensuing legal drama was everything it was predicted to be.

By December 1915, Judge Linn had issued a total of fifteen indictments, while hungry newspaper men from coast[3] to coast[4] laid bare the sordid details of what became known as Tulsa's "Vice Trust." Freeling's investigation revealed a pay-for-play scheme, by which more than a hundred establishments paid monthly "fines" to city officials, who then allowed them to trade in gambling, liquor, and prostitution.[5] In exchange for looking

---

Thomas J. Quinn, Tulsa Police Commissioner.
The "Vice Trust" was a "model" that cities such as Chicago followed after nationwide prohibition. Tulsa's elected officials such as Commissioner Quinn were simply ahead of the curve due to Oklahoma's "dry" status. The country soon caught up.
PUBLIC DOMAIN

Foster N. Burns, Tulsa Police Chief.
A former Frisco Railroad detective, Burns was appointed by Mayor Wooden who, along with Police Commissioner Quinn, fired him—twice. In return, Burns testified against his former colleagues. After the trial, he opened Burns Detective Agency and was named president of the World Association of Detectives in 1932.
BERYL FORD COLLECTION

James Woolley, Tulsa County Sheriff.
Included among the "Big Six" of the "Vice Trust" indicted in the wake of the investigation was Tulsa County Sheriff James Woolley. Not only were city and county officials implicated, but the investigation showed that national crime syndicates kept the area awash in illegal liquor.
BERYL FORD COLLECTION

the other way, the city was earning as much as $60,000 ($1.4 million in 2017 dollars) per year in allowance fines during Wooden's tenure.[6] In addition to city and county officials, the Vice Trust also included organized crime syndicates from across the United States who kept the thirsty city well stocked in return for 25 percent of liquor sales.[7]

Mayor Wooden, Police Commissioner Quinn, Police Chief Burns, and Tulsa County Sheriff James Woolley were all indicted as members of the Vice Trust's "Big Six." Also caught in the dragnet was Grant McCullough, president of the First National Bank of Tulsa, and Mayor Pro Tem O.D. Hunt. Once it became clear that the Vice Trust was doomed, members of the Big Six turned on each other, hurling scurrilous accusations of fault in every direction while boldly proclaiming their own angelic unawareness and moral outrage. Wooden and Quinn fired Chief Burns—twice[8]—and Burns, in return, became the most damning witness in both of their trials.[9] Amid the prosecutions, Hunt, who found himself as Tulsa's temporary mayor tasked with serving out what was left of Wooden's term, had a nervous breakdown and pulled a revolver on two city commissioners in the Reeder Building. Beset by a sudden irrational paranoia while raving about an unflattering editorial published about him in the *Tulsa County Chief*, Hunt threatened to kill the commissioners if they tried to attack him. He backed out of the room, gun in hand, then drove to the newspaper's production house and threatened the life of the proprietor if he printed another such article for the paper.[10]

Grant McCullough, President First National Bank.
The grand jury issued injunctions to close three alleged gambling houses and named thirteen Tulsans, ranging from prominent businessman Grant McCullough of First National Bank, to owners of the buildings and less prominent citizens. McCullough emerged unscathed and would later serve as a leader on the water commission that oversaw the Spavinaw project, personally taking the first drink of the water that flowed through the pipeline.
PUBLIC DOMAIN

DESPITE BEING *at the* CREST *of a* VICE-BUSTING WAVE, *a*
"MAYORLESS, CHIEF-*of*-POLICELESS, *and* SHERIFFLESS" TULSA RANG *in*
the 1916 NEW YEAR *as a* "VERITABLE CITY *of* JOY *and* FROLICS."

The open-town leniency practices of various administrations kept Tulsa's Red-light district and illicit speakeasies packed with high-rollers who came from all over the Magic Empire to play as hard as they worked. The money they brought with them made it easy to tip the political scales. While every politician *promised* to clean up the town, those intent on *keeping the promise* were either defeated outright, or didn't stay in office very long.   The Mayo Collection

The wild ride of "Mayor" O.D. Hunt, Tulsa's uncredited 13th chief executive.

Although you won't find his name listed on the official roster of Tulsa mayors, Oliver D. Hunt was, in fact, Tulsa's 13th mayor. In the last days of December 1915, District Judge Conn Linn removed Mayor Frank Wooden from office for corruption. As mayor pro tem, the task of filling out Wooden's remaining term fell on Hunt. Despite being caught up in the same scandal that brought down Wooden and also suffering a nervous breakdown that landed him in court for pulling a gun on his fellow commissioners, Hunt stayed at the city's helm until April 1916 when Mayor John Simmons was elected by popular vote. PUBLIC DOMAIN

Despite being at the crest of a vice-busting wave, a "mayorless, chief-of-policeless, and sheriffless" Tulsa rang in the 1916 New Year as a "veritable city of joy and frolics." Or so observed Eufaula's *Indian Journal*. According to that paper, the "frolics reigned supreme as there was not a city or county officer at the head of the legal department of either of the governments to curb the jovial crowds in their pranks."[11]

The legal complexities of removing and prosecuting so many officials set up the "greatest legal battle ever staged in Oklahoma."[12] Indeed, it would ultimately require three-and-a-half years and a ruling by the Oklahoma Supreme Court to successfully complete Mayor Wooden's prosecution. In the immediate aftermath of the initial trials, which lasted through the spring of 1916, the Republicans, with Simmons at the head of the ticket, completely swept the city elections in their first significant victory within the Democrat stronghold.

REPUBLICAN LANDSLIDE

ENTIRE TICKET ELECTED BY MAJORITIES OF 924 VOTES OR MORE

Only Democrat Elected Is Bob Purdy for School Treasurer

WEATHER REPORT
OKLAHOMA—Partly cloudy Tuesday and Wednesday.
TULSA, April 3.—The temperature: Maximum 62, minimum 39; north winds and clear.

TULSA MORNING DAILY EDITION WORLD

PROSPERITY TALK
Vote a straight Republican ticket today and you will do more to increase prosperity in Tulsa than any other one thing you could do. City government on a business basis means more prosperity.

VOL. XI, NO. 172 — TULSA, OKLAHOMA, WEDNESDAY, APRIL 5, 1916 — TEN PAGES — PRICE FIVE CENTS

SIMMONS ELECTED BY BIGGEST MAJORITY EVER RECEIVED BY CANDIDATE

CAPITAL BOOSTERS ARE COMING TODAY

Oklahoma City Business Men, 150 Strong, Arrive at 11:30 a. m.

GREEKS MAKE DEMAND AGAIN.
Request Withdrawal of Allied Troops at Saloniki.
BERLIN, April 4.—(By wireless to Sayville.)—The report that Greece has requested withdrawal of the the French and British forces at Saloniki is reiterated in an Athens dispatched received by the overseas News agency, which says the Greek government has declared the entente powers will be held responsible for further bombardment of Saloniki by German airships in case the men

SECOND CLASH LEAVES FORTY MEXICANS DEAD

JOHN H. SIMMONS
13th MAYOR of TULSA [1916-1918]

IF THERE EVER WAS A CITY needing a man in a white hat to ride into town to set things right, it was Tulsa in 1916 in the wake of the "Vice Trust" scandal. There was such a man in John H. Simmons. It was as if his résumé of government service and business experience had been pointing to Tulsa's City Hall from his boyhood days in Springfield, Missouri.

A graduate from the Henderson Academy in Webster County, Simmons taught school prior to serving four years as deputy county clerk for Wright County. His business career, which began with a Missouri bank, eventually brought him to Tulsa in 1906 as vice president of City National Bank, which merged with First National Bank in 1908. Elected to the second Oklahoma House of Representatives, Simmons returned to Tulsa as a vice president of First National Bank. He left banking for the oil business and built the Simmons Building on East 3rd Street where he became the landlord for Tulsa's powerful Chamber of Commerce. And in 1916, he led the Republican ticket to a landslide victory.

Simmons ran on a "good government ticket" that promised business-like efficiency, enforcement of vice laws, and an end to corruption. Tulsa's population doubled during Simmons's time in office, vice was managed, and the city was put back on a course of responsible leadership. Despite his popularity, Simmons's reforms proved too much for those elements who profited from Tulsa's seedy underside. Simmons and his Republican city commission were outmaneuvered in his bid for re-election.

TULSA HISTORICAL SOCIETY

Tulsa businessmen, the pride of their community, survey their boomtown from the roof of the newly completed Gallais Building (later the Kennedy Building) in April 1916.
BERYL FORD COLLECTION

Sunday morning April 2nd 1916 on Roof of Gallais Bldg

IN EARLY April 1916, Simmons and his Republican commissioners squeezed into their "dusty ill-lighted rooms"[13] in the Reeder Building. Of Simmons's accommodations, the *Morning Tulsa Daily World* observed, "The rooms are reached only by a slow-going elevator which, for a major portion of the time, refuse[s] to work. The present City Hall, however, is a part of the heritage of the previous administration and upon the shoulders of the new officials, fall[s] along with the duties and responsibilities of the offices they assumed."[14]

To help deal with the long list of badly neglected crises, Simmons was given an unquestionable mandate from the voters to fix things. Considering the gravity of all he had to deal with, it seemed unlikely that he would be at liberty to take up the matter of Tulsa's languishing City Hall any time soon. Yet a mere four days after the election, he was presented with another crisis left over from Wooden's term that would indirectly force movement on the building of a new city hall.

Tulsa in 1916.

Regardless of crime, political scandal, and the ongoing World War, Tulsa boomed its way through the mid-nineteen-teens in a way few modern Tulsans can fathom. Tulsa had tripled its population since 1910 and set the record for the fastest-growing banks in the United States. Harry Sinclair's announcement that he would anchor his $50-million oil empire to Tulsa helped propel the city's building boom and led the *Morning Tulsa Daily World* to declare "1916 is Greatest Year for Tulsa." Yet six months later, in June 1917, the paper went on to announce that Tulsa had broken the world record for building permits.

By order of the Oklahoma commissioner of charities and corrections, Tulsa's dilapidated and rat-infested city jail had finally been condemned. The state only gave Simmons until the first of June—less than two months—to replace it. It was a totally unrealistic deadline, especially considering that the funding for a new jail, which had been included in the city hall bond, had been waiting for Attorney General Freeling's signature for the previous eight months. Bond or no bond, however, building anything feasible to replace the jail in two months was impossible. But at least the urgency was enough finally to get Freeling's attention and move the bond forward.

An unexpected positive result from the timing of the jail's condemnation was that it coincided with the close of the city's fiscal year.[15] Under Simmons's push for "business-like efficiency" in the management of the city budgets, the new commissioners were able to find leftover money to fund a new jail while also providing a long-term solution for the police and fire departments and the municipal courts.[16] This meant that not only would the new city hall be free of the undesirable foot traffic that came with courts and jail cells, but that the entire $125,000 budget could go to real estate, enhanced aesthetics, and enough office space to satisfy the long-standing desire for the Chamber of Commerce to work shoulder to shoulder with city officials.

To meet the deadline of closing the jail, Simmons contracted with Tulsa County to temporarily house city prisoners at the county jail in the courthouse at 6th & Boulder.[17] To the cheers of local business owners, the old converted livery stable on 2nd Street—the same building that Wooden had hoped to expand for a city hall—was finally demolished.

With a clear picture of exactly what form the new city hall would take, and with the bonds signed and sold, all that was left was selecting a place to build. Finding a suitable lot in Tulsa's central business district was no simple matter, however. Land in America's fastest-growing boomtown was worth almost as much as the oil feeding the boom itself. Land-hungry investors, developers, and oil-titans-in-the-making were competing, checkbook in hand, for what little land was still available. Construction derricks and the steel skeletons of early high-rises had begun to punctuate every view of Tulsa's rapidly evolving skyline. Limited to sites already owned by the city, commissioners considered a lot at Archer & Boulder that was under development as a city market, and even the ballpark at Archer & Detroit. Most commissioners favored an offer to buy the Elks Club at 3rd & Boulder.[18] Even disgraced ex-Mayor Wooden tried to get in on the game. While his conviction was on appeal, he tried to broker a deal with Simmons to convert the original Christian Church building at 4th & Boulder into a city hall.[19]

Although Simmons appeared to properly consider all locations seriously suggested, he had a clear personal favorite: A prime location had come out of a very public and very ugly debate that had erupted regarding the disposition of city block 137, between 4th and 5th Streets and Boston and Cincinnati. The block had been home to Tulsa's first schoolhouse, built in

Elks Club Building, 3rd & Boulder. While Mayor Simmons was making his final decision to build a new city hall at 4th & Cincinnati, most city commissioners favored a plan to purchase the Elks Club Building for use as city offices.

1884 on a hilltop overlooking the town. The school had originally come about through the efforts of J.M. Hall to establish a Presbyterian mission to the Creek Indians. The schoolhouse was more than just a sincere desire to spread his faith; Hall also saw quality education as a fundamental building block that would have to be in place if the neophyte cowtown could ever have a real shot at becoming a decent and livable place. In 1899, Hall—with the help of Tulsa's second mayor, R.N. Bynum, and Jay Forsythe, a local rancher, banker, and Tulsa booster—transferred the school from the Presbyterian Mission Board to the new Tulsa Public

School Board, which had been founded by Hall, Bynum, and Forsythe for the occasion. Although the old Mission School had since been replaced by a large new Central High School, the community spirit attached to the Mission School had remained with the land and was still alive and well.

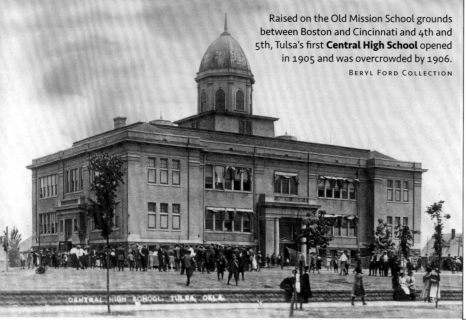

Raised on the Old Mission School grounds between Boston and Cincinnati and 4th and 5th, Tulsa's first **Central High School** opened in 1905 and was overcrowded by 1906.
BERYL FORD COLLECTION

R.N. BYNUM

2nd MAYOR of TULSA [1899-1900]

Pioneer Tulsan J.M. Hall noted that R.N. Bynum "bought Perryman and Reed's store [an early Tulsa business] in 1886, and, for many years, was a successful businessman in Tulsa." During his one term as mayor, he helped secure Tulsans' property titles, and, along with other pioneer Tulsans, loaned the city the money to start the Tulsa Public School System. BERYL FORD COLLECTION

Although barely ten years old, the new Central High School was already severely overcrowded and needed to be replaced. Only five days after the people voted on the bond to build a new city hall, the school board voted to replace Central High School. Their plan was to build a new school in a different location and offer ninety-nine-year-long leases for commercial development on the old school grounds. Buy-in for the leases would initially fund the acquisition of land elsewhere for a new school, and then, over time, provide an ongoing endowment for public education. While the board's plan was, without a doubt, the best use of their resources, they didn't consider the public outcry that would arise from the commercialization of land that was so dear to the public.

When the development plan was initially announced in an open forum, it sparked what quickly devolved into an ugly debate over whether the school board even owned block 137 or whether they were merely custodians of land that actually belonged to the City of Tulsa. Instead of commercial development on block 137, those in opposition wanted a large new school built on the southern half of the block, leaving the northern half open for development as a central park—a use they saw as appropriate for land possessed with the spirit of hope that symbolized the Tulsa that "ought to be." The passion of the debate was no doubt in part fueled by the contrast between the high-minded image of Tulsa traditionally represented by the school grounds, and the spiraling crime, vice, and indecency represented by

the red-light district that, at the time of the debate, Wooden had allowed to reinfest the old Pioneer District along 1st Street. The question would go all the way to the Oklahoma Supreme Court the following year. Ultimately, the school board won, and in September of 1916, block 137 was opened for development.

It was Tulsa oilman C.L. Holland who, in the summer of 1915, first put forth the notion that a new city hall should play a role in the development of block 137. His idea was brushed off by Mayor Wooden and Commissioner Quinn, because, in their view, the prime real estate on the school grounds was much too valuable to waste on a city hall.[20] Not surprisingly, when presented with the opportunity to acquire a lot on block 137 following the Oklahoma Supreme Court's decision, the antipodal administration of Mayor Simmons had a completely different view. He and his commissioners believed the location was "especially desirable for a city hall," because it was "convenient to the business section, and the high ground would give the municipal building a commanding position."[21]

The Municipal Building and the **Cosden Building** were under construction simultaneously. Both projects started in 1917, but, despite being nearly five times larger, the Cosden was opened two months earlier on Armistice Day, November 11, 1918.

At a Monday night meeting, on December 4, 1916, Simmons and the school board settled on an undisclosed price of about $25,001 for the southwest corner of 4th & Cincinnati. Although defeated at the Oklahoma Supreme Court, those opposed to development still had some wind left in their sails. When Simmons got word of their plans to file an injunction to block the city's purchase of the lot, he ordered City Attorney John B. Meserve to rush the transaction secretly. The day the opposition intended to file the injunction, they woke to the news that the deed had already been recorded and the property conveyed to the City of Tulsa.[22]

The Republican-leaning *Morning Tulsa Daily World*, which had heretofore ravaged proponents of development, praised Simmons for the move: "With the purchase of a site at the intersection of Fourth and Cincinnati for the erection of a municipal building, Mayor John H. Simmons and the board of city commissioners have placed the keystone into a temple of achievement which they hope will stand forever as a monument to their administration."[23]

"With the PURCHASE *of a* SITE *at the* INTERSECTION *of* FOURTH *and* CINCINNATI *for the* ERECTION *of a* MUNICIPAL BUILDING, MAYOR JOHN H. SIMMONS *and the* BOARD *of* CITY COMMISSIONERS *have* PLACED *the* KEYSTONE INTO *a* TEMPLE *of* ACHIEVEMENT WHICH THEY HOPE WILL STAND FOREVER *as a* MONUMENT *to* THEIR ADMINISTRATION."

RAISING CITY HALL

H AVING GONE THROUGH SO much effort to overcome so many setbacks, the realization that Tulsa's long-anticipated City Hall was finally becoming a reality was, in the view of Mayor Simmons and his administration, a reason to celebrate. Upon his October 1916 announcement that all the legal preparations had been finalized and the cash was in the city's strongbox, Simmons proclaimed, "It has been a long and difficult row that we have had to hoe but at last we have everything in readiness. *We are going to build a city hall!* We have the money and we surely have the desire to give the people a place as a city center which would be a beauty spot." He also announced his intention to celebrate

The Municipal Building

Southeast corner of 4th & Cincinnati. Holding a hard-to-beat record as Tulsa's longest-serving City Hall, the Municipal Building's 50 years of service to the city started with great fanfare but quickly became a matter of begrudged necessity as Tulsa outgrew the building but couldn't afford its dream of a Civic Center.

PUBLIC DOMAIN

New City Hall, Tulsa, Okla.

HAND-COLORED

the groundbreaking with a "special event of no little interest," complete with an automobile parade featuring civic and industrial delegates.[1]

To design the building, he secured the services of local architects Rush, Endacott & Rush. Seven months later, the firm delivered a set of plans that would become one of the most important transitional works of the father-and-son team of A.W. Rush and E.A. Rush. Their design for what they entitled the "Municipal Building" helped move them from their earlier rusticated stone Romanesque revival public buildings to the more dramatic and diverse Neoclassical, Beaux-Arts, and Art Deco styles of commercial architecture for which they are best remembered. When the plans were made public on March 2, 1917,[2] Rush, Endacott & Rush's vision for the Municipal Building was hailed as the "finest to be found in the state."[3]

As Simmons had promised, the plan provided for a four-story building, with space enough to house all the city offices (apart from the police, fire, courts, and jail, which had, the previous year, settled into their new building on 2nd Street) under one roof alongside the Retail Merchants' Association, the park and school boards, and, naturally, the Chamber of Commerce. In fact, in his *History of Tulsa, Oklahoma*, Colonel Clarence B. Douglas directly credited Mayor Simmons's administration for having included, designed, and dedicated the fourth floor "in recognition of the services the Chamber of Commerce has render[ed] to the city."[4] In addition to the Chamber's offices, the floor also included a six-hundred-seat civic auditorium that served as a popular meeting place for events too small for Convention Hall. To the excitement and surprise of Tulsa's newspapermen, the new Municipal Building would also, "in true metropolitan style," include desk space reserved for daily ink slingers.

As was common for the day, the building came along with a promise of being "fireproof" due to its skeleton of steel instead of wood. The interior public spaces were to be finished with white enameled brick flooring. A grand white-marble stairway would connect a split-level lobby off of the main 4th Street entrance to the first and second floors, where the public would do most of its business. All of the interior stairs and banisters promised ornamented ironwork, and in what would become a painful sticking point *(see page 71)*, the generous use of white-marble wainscoting was also specified throughout the building.

The most notable feature of the design were ten fluted and engaged Ionic columns spanning the 4th Street frontage between the second and third floors. The ten columns, a number chosen to represent the justice and authority of the Ten Commandments, were the dominant feature that defined the building's Neoclassical style, and it successfully made the profound statement of authoritative and competent governance that the idealists among Tulsa's leadership had worked so hard to achieve in the short but remarkably eventful twenty-three years since the incident at the Archer Store.

TEN FLUTED *and* ENGAGED IONIC COLUMNS *were the* DOMINANT FEATURE SUCCESSFULLY MAKING *the* PROFOUND STATEMENT *of* AUTHORITATIVE *and* COMPETENT GOVERNANCE *the* IDEALISTS AMONG TULSA'S LEADERSHIP *had* WORKED SO HARD *to* ACHIEVE.

MUNICIPAL BUILDING

WEST ELEVATION

LONGITUDINAL SECTION

SECTION THRU FRONT WALL

EXTERIOR DETAILS

WINDOW DETAILS

JAMB

HEAD

MEETING

SILL

STONE

PLASTER

GRADE

CITY COMMISSIONERS OFFICE - NORTH

MAYORS OFFICE - SOUTH

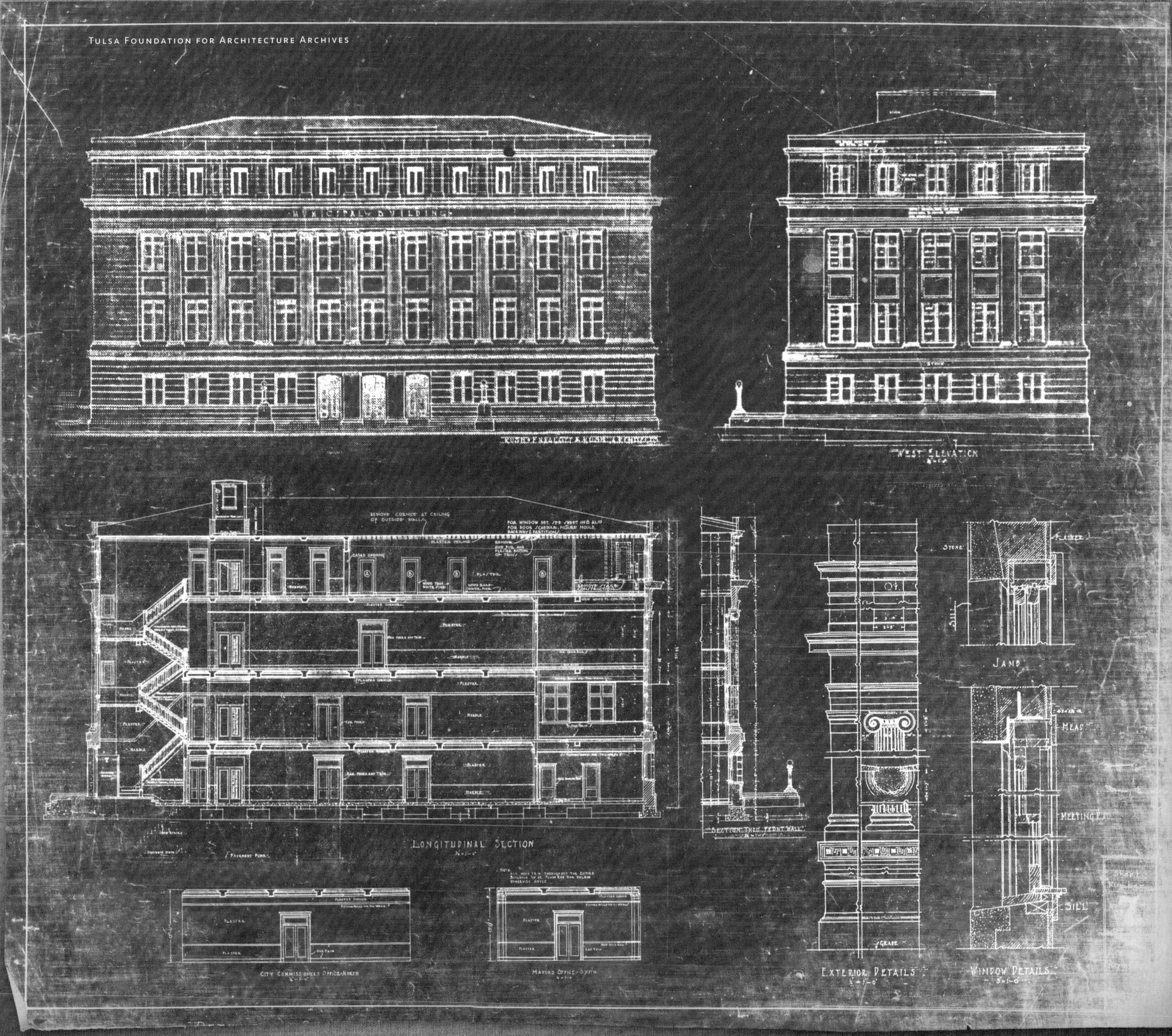

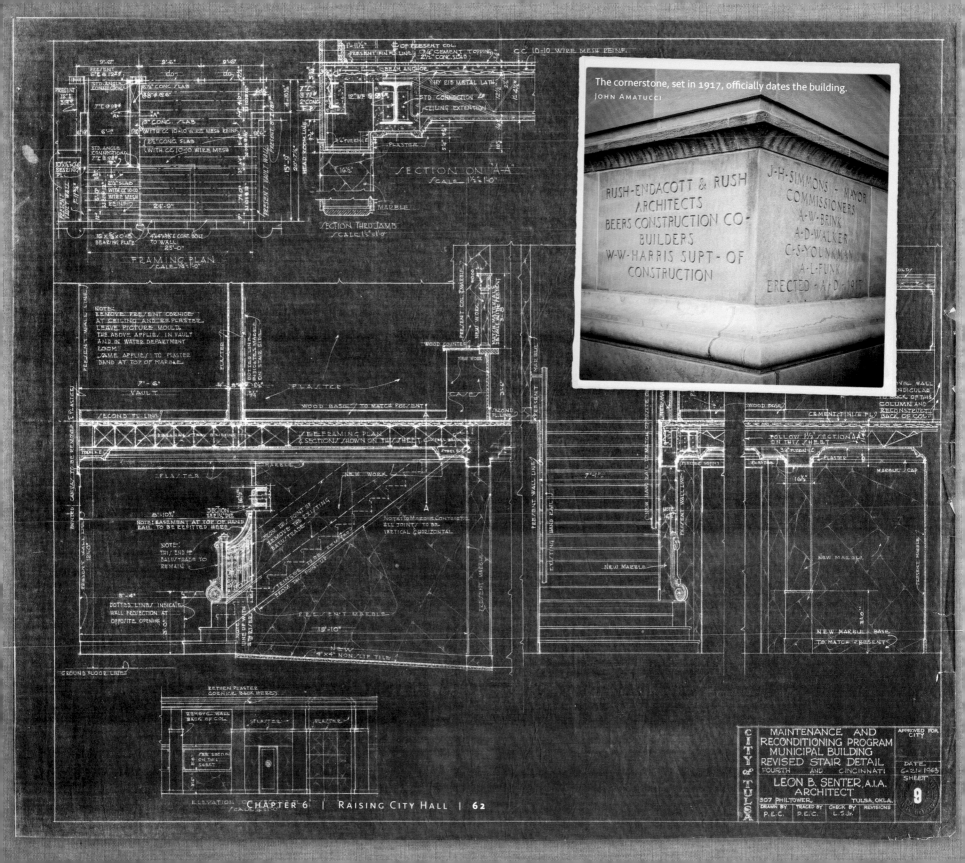

The cornerstone, set in 1917, officially dates the building.
John Amatucci

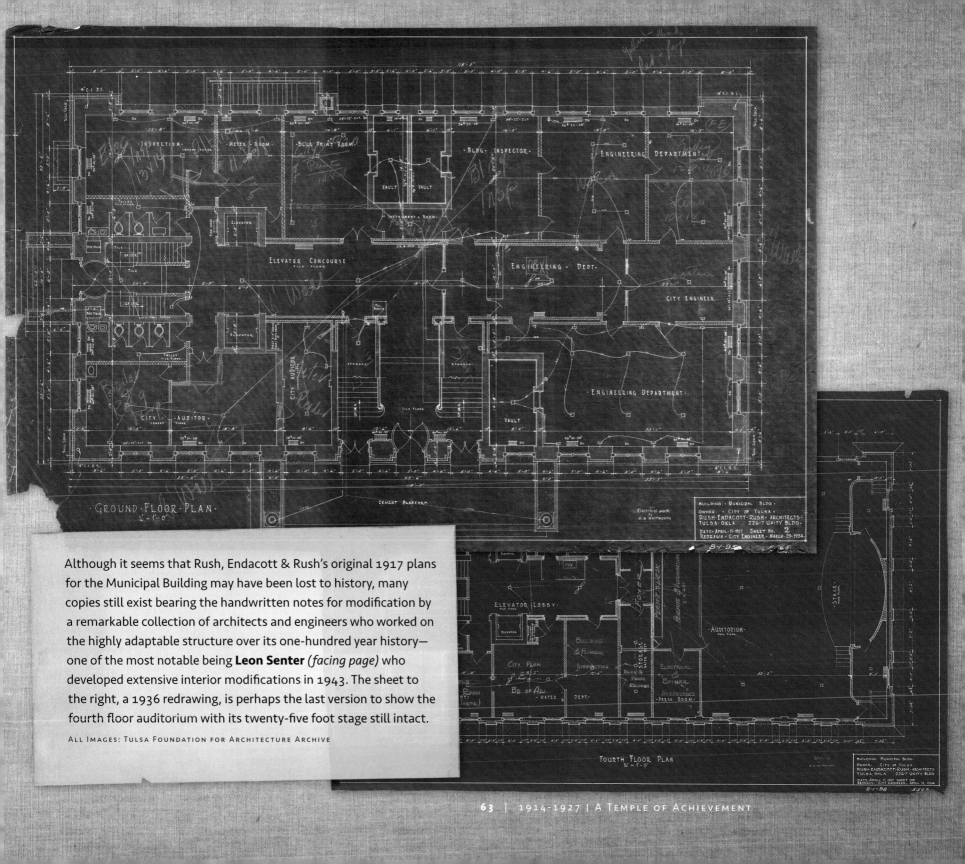

Although it seems that Rush, Endacott & Rush's original 1917 plans for the Municipal Building may have been lost to history, many copies still exist bearing the handwritten notes for modification by a remarkable collection of architects and engineers who worked on the highly adaptable structure over its one-hundred year history—one of the most notable being **Leon Senter** *(facing page)* who developed extensive interior modifications in 1943. The sheet to the right, a 1936 redrawing, is perhaps the last version to show the fourth floor auditorium with its twenty-five foot stage still intact.

Rush, Endacott & Rush

The Municipal Building became a transitional hallmark that would help elevate the careers of the architects who created it.

The design of Tulsa's Municipal Building was an unlikely solution for a firm that, while well known for designing public buildings, was clearly trying new things. And while the building did not reflect the previous work of Rush, Endacott & Rush, it also looked little like any of their subsequent work either. Little more than a decade later, they completed the project that would set the firm's name in stone: The Boston Avenue Methodist Church. And no two buildings in Tulsa could be less alike.

Founded before the turn of the century by father and son William and Arthur Rush in Grand Rapids, the firm moved to Chicago in 1910 where they became practiced in the Chicago School of Architecture that was influenced by Chicago greats like Louis Sullivan and Henry Hobson Richardson. In 1912, under the name E.A. Rush (Arthur's initials) & Company, the company came to a booming Tulsa and added Asbury Endacott as a partner in 1915—becoming Rush, Endacott & Rush. Endacott was the structural engineer of the firm. His political aspirations also contributed to securing business opportunities for the firm. He was elected water commissioner in 1928, and ran unsuccessfully for mayor in 1932.

He also was chief construction engineer for the water and sewer plants at Mohawk Park.

The Municipal Building was a departure from the Rushes' early work in rusticated stone structures for which the firm was well known. Their Tulsa work reflected the evolution of popular Beaux-Arts, Neoclassical, and neo-Gothic styles. By the later half of the 1920s, the firm quickly adapted to the Art Deco movement with their hallmark work on the Tulsa Building, the Page Warehouse, and, most notably, the Boston Avenue Methodist Church.

A contributing factor to the dynamic evolution of the firm was a young prodigy named Bruce Goff. Goff began an apprenticeship with the firm at only 11 years old after his father grew tired of his son wasting paper drawing buildings. While Goff's talent was immediately recognized by the firm, it is doubtful that he played any role other than observer during the firm's Municipal Building project.

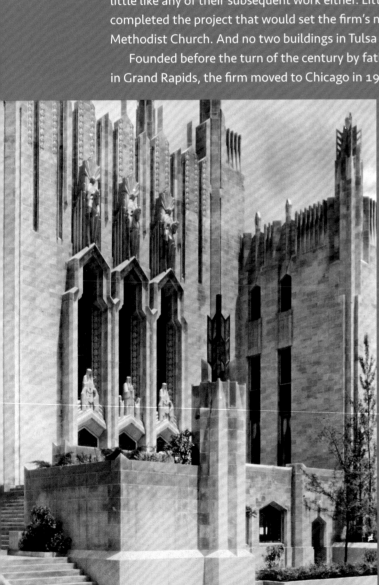

Boston Avenue Methodist-Episcopal Church, exterior, Tulsa, OK, 1926. Bruce Goff and Rush, Endacott & Rush, architects. HISTORIC ARCHITECTURE AND LANDSCAPE IMAGE COLLECTION, RYERSON AND BURNHAM ARCHIVES, THE ART INSTITUTE OF CHICAGO. DIGITAL FILE #30444

The diversity of styles that followed the Municipal Building can be seen in Rush, Endacott & Rush's design for the Beaux-Arts 1922 **Atlas Life Building** (right) and the Art Deco 1929 Tulsa Building (below). BERYL FORD COLLECTION

MAYOR SIMMONS, the city commissioners, and especially the Chamber of Commerce fell in love with the architects' vision for the Municipal Building. Both the timing of the project and the design of the building represented the perfect allegory of Tulsa's government rising from the ashes of corruption and dysfunction into a new era of strength, stability, and competent authority. Fortunately, the voters of Tulsa also fell in love with the architects' vision, because, when the bids for construction came in at the end of May 1917, they were not even close to being within budget.

After the purchase of the land, the city only had about $102,000 left to complete the project. The construction estimates alone—not including finishing and furnishing—came in at between $113,268 and $149,700.[5] The most realistic estimate for fully executing Rush, Endacott & Rush's vision was closer to $175,000—a startling number when compared to the $20,000 that Wooden had suggested for his original plan a mere two years earlier.

Fortunately, apart from his civic duties as mayor, John Simmons was also a successful property developer, well recognized for his skill and acumen. In fact, during the same time that he was developing the Municipal Building, he was also considering raising his own narrow skyscraper on the north side of 3rd Street between Boston and Cincinnati, where he already owned the Simmons Building.[6] A small but prestigious address tucked neatly between the ten-story Daniel Building and the famous Hotel Tulsa, also ten stories at that point,[7] the Simmons Building was an attractive three-story edifice finished in graceful terra-cotta ornamentation. It was best known around Tulsa as the home to Simmons' largest tenant—the Chamber of Commerce.

Applying his skill as a developer, Mayor Simmons negotiated an alternate deal with the contractor deemed best suited for the project, the Beers Construction Company of Tulsa. In exchange for being awarded the contract, Beers would lower its bid to $102,600,[8] while Simmons went to the voters for a second bond request of $75,000. Beers agreed to assume the risk that the second bond might not pass. Their only stipulation was that the contract exclude the finishing millwork, elevators, seats for the auditorium, and vault files. The deal was struck, and Beers was awarded the contract on June 6, 1917.

Simmons felt confident in assuming that the additional $75,000 would be easy to come up with, because he and his commissioners had already been hard at work on a million-dollar infrastructure request that was, at the time, already the largest bond request in the history of Tulsa. His assumption that voters would scarcely notice the addition of

Despite its modest size, the **Simmons Building** (*second from the right*) was one of Tulsa's most prestigious addresses. Home of the powerful Chamber of Commerce before it moved into the Municipal Building in 1919, it was toppled along with the Daniel Building and Hotel Tulsa to make room for the Williams Center, c.1972. BERYL FORD COLLECTION

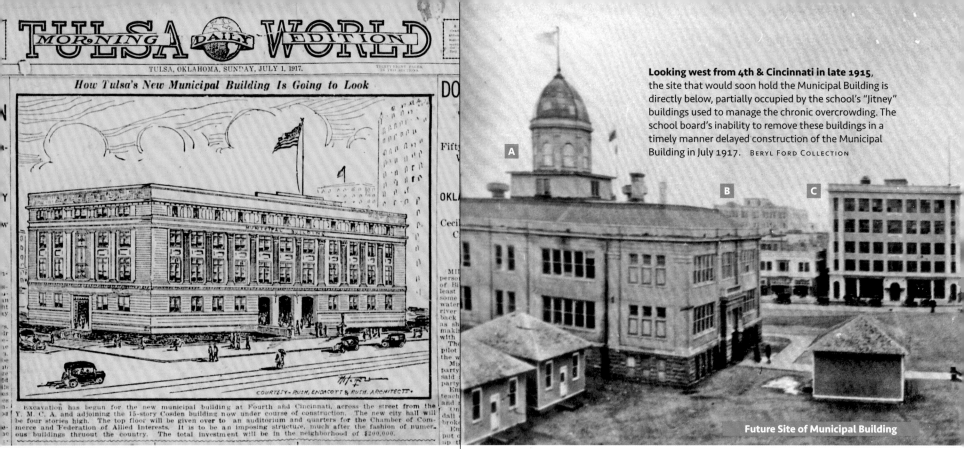

COURTESY · RUSH, ENDACOTT & RUSH, ARCHITECTS

How Tulsa's New Municipal Building Is Going to Look

TULSA, OKLAHOMA, SUNDAY, JULY 1, 1917.

Excavation has begun for the new municipal building at Fourth and Cincinnati, across the street from the Y. M. C. A. and adjoining the 15-story Cosden building now under course of construction. The new city hall will be four stories high. The top floor will be given over to an auditorium and quarters for the Chamber of Commerce and Federation of Allied Interests. It is to be an imposing structure, much after the fashion of numerous buildings thruout the country. The total investment will be in the neighborhood of $200,000.

Looking west from 4th & Cincinnati in late 1915, the site that would soon hold the Municipal Building is directly below, partially occupied by the school's "Jitney" buildings used to manage the chronic overcrowding. The school board's inability to remove these buildings in a timely manner delayed construction of the Municipal Building in July 1917. BERYL FORD COLLECTION

Future Site of Municipal Building

Plans for an "automobile parade" celebrating the new Municipal Building groundbreaking were delayed to the point that this three-column, front-page rendering by **Rush, Endacott & Rush** published in the July 1, 1917 edition of the *Morning Tulsa Daily World* was the only celebration given to the long-awaited event. It would be the first of many delays.

more money for the Municipal Building was proven correct when the package passed with virtually no opposition on July 11, 1917.

Before the bond had even been voted on, the "City Dads," as newspapermen liked to refer to Tulsa's leadership, were so confident in its passage, so enthusiastic about their new Municipal Building, and so anxious to escape the Reeder Building,

that they extended a carrot-and-stick offer to the Beers Company to hit an exceptionally aggressive opening date of February 1, 1918. The offer included a bonus of $13 for each day Beers finished ahead of schedule and a loss of $13 for every day they ran behind.[9]

As it turned out, Beers should not have taken the deal.

A harbinger of what would become a long list of troubles and delays that Beers would endure during the construction of the Municipal Building came when the grand parade to celebrate the groundbreaking fell victim to the school board's inability to remove their temporary classroom buildings from the lot on schedule.[10] Excavation on the site couldn't start until the first week of July 1917—about three weeks late. Instead of a parade, Simmons's celebration was downgraded to an attractive rendering of the building printed with a brief, five-line announcement on the front page of the July 1, 1917, edition of the *Morning Tulsa Daily World*.[11] As the project moved along, the

A) **Old Central School,** demolished 1922 for Atlas Life Building; B) **Mayo Building,** 5th & Main, still standing; C) **Pioneer Telephone Company Building,** demolished 1966, now 400 Boston Building; D) **Palace Building,** 4th & Main, still standing; E) **Clinton Building,** demolished 1927, now south end of 320 South Boston Building; F) **Gallais Building,** still standing as south side of Kennedy Building; G) **YMCA,** demolished 1954, now Fourth Street Parking garage; H) **Daniel Building,** demolished 1973, now part of Williams Center Plaza; I) **Hotel Tulsa,** demolished 1972, now the Performing Arts Center; J) **Triangle Building,** still standing.

difficulties in securing manpower and materials amid the ongoing war in Europe proved so difficult that the February 1st deadline would come and go with hardly a mention.

Part of Simmons's plan in rushing the construction was to time the Municipal Building's grand opening with the launch of his re-election bid. Tulsa voters would return to the polls in April 1918. A completed Municipal Building would be a perfect, high-visibility manifestation of the record of achievement boasted by Simmons and his commissioners.

Even though the Municipal Building was nowhere near completion at the launch of his campaign, no one had any reason to expect anything other than a Sunday afternoon stroll to victory for Simmons. Not only did he have an outstanding record, but he was also popular and well-liked by the progressive-minded elements of the business community, as well as the law-and-order voters. His opponent, on the other hand, was a mystery to most

Tulsans. A recent transplant to the city, Charles H. Hubbard had spent the entire campaign confined to a hospital bed in Kansas City with a paralyzing ailment that was never fully explained to the public. Yet, given the fickle nature of Tulsa's electorate, no candidate from either party could ever assume he was totally safe.

As it turned out, the Republicans could have used whatever enthusiasm a finished Municipal Building might have drummed up. No sooner did voters start shuffling into the polls on the morning of April 2, 1918, than it became clear that Simmons and his "Good Government" ticket was in serious trouble.[12]

The Municipal Building shortly after opening in 1919. Directly behind the building *(far left)* can be seen the War Savings Bank. The War Bond Building, as it was commonly known, had been recently moved to make room for the Hunt Building at 4th & Main.
Tulsa Historical Society

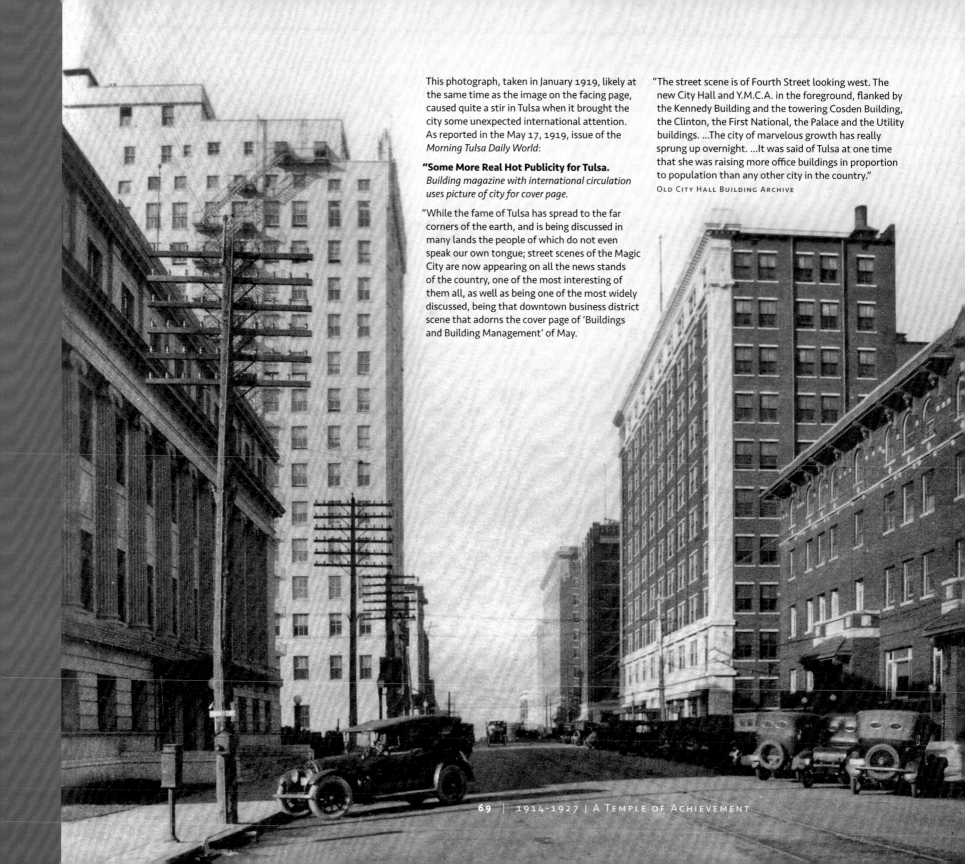

This photograph, taken in January 1919, likely at the same time as the image on the facing page, caused quite a stir in Tulsa when it brought the city some unexpected international attention. As reported in the May 17, 1919, issue of the *Morning Tulsa Daily World*:

"Some More Real Hot Publicity for Tulsa.
Building magazine with international circulation uses picture of city for cover page.

"While the fame of Tulsa has spread to the far corners of the earth, and is being discussed in many lands the people of which do not even speak our own tongue; street scenes of the Magic City are now appearing on all the news stands of the country, one of the most interesting of them all, as well as being one of the most widely discussed, being that downtown business district scene that adorns the cover page of 'Buildings and Building Management' of May.

"The street scene is of Fourth Street looking west. The new City Hall and Y.M.C.A. in the foreground, flanked by the Kennedy Building and the towering Cosden Building, the Clinton, the First National, the Palace and the Utility buildings. ...The city of marvelous growth has really sprung up overnight. ...It was said of Tulsa at one time that she was raising more office buildings in proportion to population than any other city in the country."
OLD CITY HALL BUILDING ARCHIVE

Charles H. Hubbard
14*th* Mayor *of* Tulsa [1918-1920]

Historians identify Charles H. Hubbard as "an oil driller and a staunch Democrat" who upset Mayor Simmons's bid for re-election, and was the only Tulsa mayor sworn into office in his bedroom. Mysteriously ill and out of public view during the entire campaign, Hubbard was apparently still suffering as a legally dubious oath was administered behind closed doors at Hubbard's home, 310 E. 10th Street. Despite a prohibition on visitors, Mrs. Hubbard said the new mayor was "doing splendidly." The hallmark of Hubbard's administration was having to shut down the city to try to stop the spread of the "Spanish Influenza" that killed 7,359 Oklahomans. Public Domain

In addition to doing a competent job of running the city, Mayor Simmons, like Mayor Martin before him, had, indeed, lived up to his closed-town promises of keeping vice and corruption at bay. Or at least he had sincerely engaged in the battle to do so. While not a part of the Democratic machine's public agenda, it was well understood that if Hubbard was elected, Tulsa would return to its status as an open town, with more leniency in the enforcement of prohibitory laws. With that as their rallying cry, Tulsa's "Wet" Democrats quietly organized, then swamped the polls while Simmons's law-and-order Republicans, so confident in their assumption of an easy victory, didn't bother to vote. With scarcely more than 4 percent of Tulsans participating in the election, the baffled electorate who had stayed home opened their morning papers the next day to learn that their popular mayor, along with every one of his Republican reformers on the City Commission, had been easily swept from power.

Following the impeachment of Mayor Wooden, Simmons had come into office on the back of Tulsa's first acting mayor, O.D. Hunt. He would leave his office in the questionable hands of Tulsa's second acting mayor, Martin J. McNulty Jr. Following a legally dubious transition of power conducted by the city attorney and city auditor, who passed handwritten notes to and from the still-bedridden and sequestered Mayor-Elect Hubbard, McNulty voted for himself to accept Tulsa's fourteenth mayorship on Hubbard's behalf.[13]

True to the nature of a Greek tragedy suited to match the columns on the Municipal Building, John Simmons would never enjoy the beautiful oak-paneled executive chambers in the building he had been so instrumental in raising. Simmons's absence hung like a pall over the duration of the building project, which dragged on through the strange and rocky start to Mayor Hubbard's term. In June, a power struggle in the office of the building inspector resulted in yet more delays.[14] Simmons's inspector, Courtland

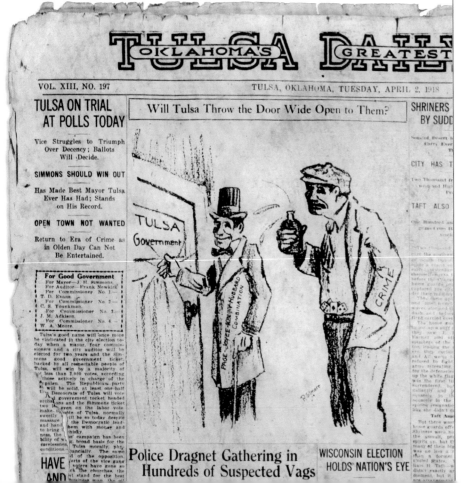

L. Butler, who had overseen the project since its inception, was forced out. Hubbard's replacement for him, J.M. Whiteside, began ordering changes,[15] and, by August, the city engineer and city attorney were at odds with Beers Construction regarding cost overruns that continued a steady march toward the $200,000 mark.[16] A new October deadline failed to materialize, along with the promised delivery of the marble needed to complete the interior wainscoting, stairs, and ornamentation. After a series of threats by the city, the Carthage, Missouri, marble quarry finally confessed that they were still months away from fulfilling the order. With progress at a virtual standstill by the end of 1918, the city and the Chamber of Commerce decided to make the best of the situation.

As if in mourning, the building itself refused its own grand opening as it begrudgingly went into operation exactly one year to the day beyond the opening date originally set by Mayor Simmons. Not only was it a year late and over budget, it opened with absolutely no fanfare due to its incomplete state. What ultimately proved to be a five-month delay in receiving the marble, required that the building be slowly and unceremoniously occupied, one department at a time, starting with the Chamber of Commerce on February 1, 1919.[17] It wasn't until the beginning of April of that year[18] that marble fitters were able to replace the rough-hewn boards serving as stair treads and truly "finish" the Municipal Building with the gleaming white elegance originally envisioned by Rush, Endacott & Rush.

DESPITE THE lack of festivities connected to its opening, the Municipal Building was, once it was truly finished, quickly embraced by the public and broadly celebrated by the Chamber of Commerce. It garnered international attention on the May 1919 cover of the prestigious magazine *Buildings and Building Management*, and it became a focal point promoted by the Chamber of Commerce as a symbol of everything they wanted outsiders to see in Tulsa. To underscore this intention, the city had commissioned an enormous seventeen-by-five-foot mural on canvas to hang above the front doors inside the main lobby facing 4th Street.

The mural, originally entitled *Tulsa, Her Past and Future*, was the work of a nationally known portraitist and muralist named William R. Steene. Described by the *Morning Tulsa Daily World* as "beautiful beyond description, and just the finishing touch absolutely necessary to the new city hall," the mural presented an allegory of Tulsa in the form of a beautiful young maiden adorned in royal robes sitting upon a throne surrounded by symbols of wealth and success. A small child symbolizing Tulsa's future offers her a golden oil well on a silver salver in exchange for the crown of laurels she is holding out to him. Three powerful figures—representing industry, agriculture, and education—stand to the side, waiting to serve the child as he grows.[19]

TULSA, HER PAST *and* FUTURE

by *William R. Steene*
1918

LOST ALONG WITH THE MURAL that adorned the lobby of the Municipal Building was the painting's original title, "Tulsa, Her Past and Future." Known today as "An Allegory of Tulsa," the new name is apt in more than just an expression of its subject matter. The history of the mural itself has turned out to be a fitting allegory of the Municipal Building's own history.

American painter William R. Steene (1887-1965) had already established himself as a portraitist and muralist by the time he was commissioned in 1918 to paint for Tulsa's new City Hall. Having studied at Fontainebleau School of Art and under Colarossi and Julian in Paris, Steene and his new wife, Eula Mae, came to Tulsa in search of opportunity at the time the Municipal Building was under construction.

Eula Mae was a stage actress when William met her while painting backdrops. Their second daughter, Marianne, who went on to become a famous golden-age fashion model and Warner Bros. actress, was born in Tulsa less than a month after the mural was unveiled. As she grew in stature and beauty, her face became a familiar feature in many of her father's later paintings. Interestingly, the figure of "Miss Tulsa" in the Municipal Building's mural bares an undeniable resemblance to the woman Marianne would become, suggesting that her mother likely modeled for the piece.

Steene was paid $750 for his work, which is equivalent to about $10,000 in 2017 dollars. According to the city, the extra expense was "absolutely necessary" to "create an additional atmosphere of dignity about the new City Hall and complete the finishing touch."

Like the Municipal Building, Steene's beautiful work was well-received by the public when it was unveiled in the spring of 1919. But also like the Municipal Building,

the years took a heavy toll, and, by the time the city moved to its new home in the Civic Center 50 years later, the value of the mural was long forgotten.

Upon its departure in May 1969, the city took everything it considered worth salvaging, leaving the rest to be liquidated by public auction. The once-adored mural, plastered into place on the lobby wall and badly stained by years of tobacco smoke, dust, and neglect, was among the items left behind.

Despite the best efforts of the Williams Auction Company, the mural did not receive a single bid. It seems the daunting challenge of removing it from the wall outweighed anyone's interest in the famous painting. At the end of the day, the auctioneer, W.D. "Bill" Williams and his wife, OawEtta, decided they liked the mural enough to purchase it for themselves. The price they paid to acquire the piece turned out to be about $12 to the City of Tulsa and one broken arm suffered by Bill's assistant when the surprising weight of the plaster-infused canvas knocked him off the ladder during its removal.

Whatever plans the Williamses had for the mural were never realized as it sat rolled up in storage for the next 38 years—coincidentally, the same period of time City Hall stayed at the Civic Center. While in storage, the canvas began to collapse under its own weight and might have been lost forever had the auctioneer's sons not had the unconventional but effective idea of patching it with duct tape. Having inherited the mural with the eventual passing of their parents, the sons realized it needed a proper home. Upon their decision to auction it in 2008, a friend of a private art collector in Tulsa became aware of the sale and, without any more explanation than, "you'll know it when you see it," urged the collector to attend the auction. As expected, the collector "knew it when he saw it" and immediately fell in love with the piece.

Realizing its true value, he sent the mural to Van Witt Fine Art Conservation in Overland Park, Kansas, for a complete restoration. Working in a large warehouse, Peggy Van Witt and her team carefully removed more than 15 pounds of plaster particles, cleaned and sealed the original surface and skillfully painted-in the scratches and scars with conservation paints that matched Steene's original work. Finally, they lined the restored canvas on specially made acid-free panels that will protect the work from further decay. At nearly 100 years of age, the mural remains safe and appreciated in private ownership.

Below: Empty marble frame where the mural once hung as it appeared in 1973. Today the spot is covered by a new mural (see page 124). *Left:* Van Witt's team works on restoration.

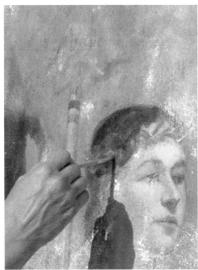

ABOVE: VAN WITT FINE ART CONSERVATION
RIGHT: OLD CITY HALL BUILDING ARCHIVE

The mural and the Municipal Building in which it hung were romanticized fulfillments of the vision held for Tulsa by J.M. Hall, Reverend Mowbray, and so many other founding fathers who sincerely believed that their Magic City could be everything they advertised it to be. And in a great many ways—most ways, actually—Tulsa *was* everything it was advertised to be. At the time of the Municipal Building's opening, the power of Tulsa's commerce had built a 90,000-person-strong empire of the common man filled with beautiful schools, libraries, houses of worship, parks, and homes. Oil was still fueling the dreams and fortunes of many who stumbled into town with little more than their ambition and their work ethic. Even those whom the period's cultural bigotries conspired to suppress found their own slice of the Magic City.

In another great twist in Tulsa's ironic history, Mayor Rohde's adoption of the state's Jim Crow laws created a closed-market system for Tulsa's African-American Greenwood District, into which income from the region's thriving economy flowed both quickly and one way. Once in Greenwood, black dollars circulated through black-owned businesses and churches with compounding speed and volume, creating one of the nation's most remarkable centers for black affluence.

For as good and prosperous as Tulsa was above the waterline, Hubbard's migration back to open-city policies allowed its underside to remain chronically plagued by crime and vice—and the violent unrest wrought by the bad seeds that inevitably came with it. In the spring of 1921, during the peak of one of Tulsa's most bountiful periods, the city fell victim to a growing national trend of racial unrest. A steady diet of scurrilous reporting from the former *Tulsa Democrat*, newly reorganized as the *Tulsa Tribune*, helped incite what famed civil rights activist Walter F. White explained as "a bitter resentment on the part of the lower order of whites"[20] against the success of Greenwood. There will always be those who rationalize the woes of their own lives by placing fault on the success of others. Such was the underlying attitude of bitterness, bigotry, and jealousy on the night of May 30, 1921, when a politically and socially motivated mob of working-class whites rioted and reduced more than thirty-five blocks in Greenwood to ashes and left hundreds of their African-American neighbors dead, with thousands more homeless.

Mayor T.D. Evans signing the Bond for the Spavinaw Water Project in the Municipal Building, June 21, 1921. *Back row, standing left to right:* E.D. Short *(City Treasurer)*, Charles Griggs *(City Engineer); next row,* Frank Duncan *(City Attorney)*, Lilah D. Lindsay, O.A. Steiner *(Street Commissioner)*, Dollie Nelson, Grant McCullough, H.F. Newblock *(Finance Commissioner)*, C.S. Younkman *(Water Commissioner)*, C.S. Avery, Eugene Lorton, W.R. Holway *(Chief of Engineers of Project)*, J.M. Atkinson *(Police Commissioner). Seated left to right:* Mrs. S.R. Lewis, Mrs. J. Benjamin Brown, T.D. Evans *(Mayor)*, Mrs. Frank Seaman *(City Auditor)*.
TULSA HISTORICAL SOCIETY

Spavinaw Water Project.

As Tulsa boomed, well water and imported bottled water could not meet the demand. After two decades of trial and error—with no expense spared—failed to adequately separate Arkansas River water from Arkansas River mud, two competing plans evolved to solve Tulsa's chronic water woes. Shell Creek in Sand Springs was heavily promoted as a clean water source by Charles Page, but once its supply was deemed inadequate, city engineer T.C. Hughes studied topographic maps and concluded that water from Spavinaw Creek in Mayes County could supply Tulsa via gravity flow. With the construction of 55 miles of pipeline, clean water came to Tulsa in 1924.

B.C. FRANKLIN
The SAVIOR *of* GREENWOOD

In an overt attempt to prevent the rebuilding of Tulsa's Black Wall Street, Mayor Evans and the city commission approved an extension of city fire codes that would make it nearly impossible for Tulsans who had lost everything to rebuild their homes and businesses in Greenwood. Within three days, however, Attorney B.C. Franklin, with the aid of I.H. Spears and T.O. Chappelle, filed suit against the City of Tulsa in district court. Franklin argued that the end result of the ordinance would be a virtual seizure of land apart from due process of law. On September 1, 1921, three district judges agreed with Franklin and declared Mayor Evans's fire codes to be unconstitutional. By fighting for this pivotal decision and thus securing the promise of a prosperous Greenwood for the next two generations, B.C. Franklin proved that, even in the face of insurmountable odds, you *can* fight City Hall.

Looking north on Greenwood from Archer, 1938. Overcoming tremendous obstacles and opposition, Greenwood courageously recovered from almost total destruction within five years of the Tulsa Race Riot. It went on to reach the peak of its prosperity 16 years later in 1941. At the time this photo was taken in 1938, Deep Greenwood was home to some 400 businesses. Tulsa Historical Society

Aftermath of the Burning of Greenwood, 1921. An African-American man with his camera surveys the skeletons of iron beds which rise above the ashes of a burned-out block.

The following morning found the entire administration of T.D. Evans, Tulsa's fifteenth mayor and the successor to Mayor Hubbard, barricaded and paralyzed inside the Municipal Building. An incensed Loyal J. Martin, having become a district judge since his time as mayor, confronted city officials in an irate swearing match in the third floor Commission Room. In his autobiography, Martin stated that, after deriding them for their incompetence and inaction, he called more than forty of Tulsa's business leaders to the fourth-floor auditorium for an emergency meeting, in which, according to Martin, "I went after the mayor and the commissioners as hard as I could, told them they had fallen down on the job, that they had disgraced the city, that they should get out and get someone else to take charge of the city."[21] In response to Martin's efforts, the powerful business community established a committee that effectively supplanted Tulsa's municipal authority until recovery efforts in Greenwood had begun.[22]

The burning of Greenwood left wounds from which Tulsa will never fully recover. Despite it all, however, the seemingly unending oil boom continued without interruption. The ongoing economic boom and growth of Tulsa bolstered a spirit of proud indomitability with which the courageous Greenwood community rebuilt itself against every odd and much opposition—even from some elements of the black community. In one of the nation's single most powerful and inspirational feats of overcoming racial injustice, Greenwood defiantly roared back into being and prospered for another thirty years.[23]

Nineteen twenty-five was a banner year for Tulsa. Greenwood was bigger and more prosperous than it had been before the riot, and with the completion of the Spavinaw Water System, all of Tulsa was finally drinking the sparking clean water it had been promised for nearly twenty years. "Uncle Herman" Newblock, Tulsa's sixteenth mayor, was halfway through his three-term run at the job—the longest to date in Tulsa's turbulent political history.

T.D. EVANS
15th MAYOR of TULSA [1920-1922]

Thaddeus D. Evans was a native Iowan and a farm loan banker who returned the mayor's office to the Republican party in 1920. Evans's grand failure and grand achievement both came in June 1921 when he first led the city's disastrous handling of the 1921 Race Riot, then secured funding for the remarkable Spavinaw Water Project. Both events continue to have a dramatic impact on the city that Tulsa is today. Public Domain

HERMAN F. NEWBLOCK
16*th* MAYOR *of* TULSA [1922-1928]
19*th* MAYOR *of* TULSA [1932-1934]

Affectionately known in his second mayoral term as "Uncle Herman," Herman Newblock was a lawman (Tulsa's first chief of police in 1908, and later Tulsa County sheriff), city finance commissioner under two mayors, one of the city's longest-serving mayors, and one of only two mayors to hold office for two separate terms. In 1922, he defeated a political newcomer who replaced incumbent Mayor Evans on the Republican side of the city ticket. Over the years, the Arkansas-native dealt in real estate as a sideline. He was a strong supporter of the Spavinaw Water Project.

The only downside to the growth and prosperity was a problem that every other public institution in Tulsa knew all too well—both City Hall and the Chamber of Commerce were already rapidly outgrowing their new Municipal Building.

Before the Municipal Building had even celebrated its fourth birthday, both the city and the Chamber were already weighing their options. Neither body came out of the 1921 riot nearly so chummy with the other, and both were running out of space. A split was inevitable, and in April 1922, plans for a separation began to surface, with both sides viewing the Municipal Building as the booby prize.

When the Chamber began a high-pressure funding drive for the construction of a new home for itself, the Tulsa Real Estate Exchange suggested a plan in which Tulsa County, also in need of more space, would build a new courthouse and City Hall would take over the courthouse at 5th & Boulder, leaving the Municipal Building for the Chamber's use.[24] The Chamber, however, had a much bigger vision for itself—one that wouldn't fit in the Municipal Building. By the end of the year, they had twisted the arms of every businessman in the city to acquire the needed funding for what they termed their "Civic Center"—a combined hall for all of Tulsa's commercial organizations. The Chamber signed a ninety-nine-year lease with Tulsa Public Schools for the last available lot on block 137—the northwest corner of 5th & Cincinnati. And in 1925, they engaged the services of Rush, Endacott & Rush to design an eleven-story streamlined Art Deco masterpiece they called the "Tulsa Building." Known today as the Tulsa Club Building, it opened in December 1927.

Even with the space vacated by the Chamber, the Municipal Building was much too small for Tulsa's rapidly expanding government. A new solution was urgently needed. The following spring, Tulsans elected a determined new mayor who had a vision for replacing the Municipal Building with a center of government power that would make the Chamber's opulent new home look positively modest.

Tulsa Building, 1927. Designed ten years after the Municipal Building by the same firm, Rush, Endacott & Rush, the eleven-story Tulsa Club Building shows the remarkable influence young architect Bruce Goff had on the otherwise traditional firm. The building was a joint effort of the Chamber of Commerce and the Tulsa Club, which was founded in 1925. For decades it reigned as the meeting place for Tulsa's elite. A victim of changing times, the Tulsa Club folded in 1994, and the building fell into tragic disrepair. In 2017, Tulsa's Ross Group began a complete restoration project that included a luxury hotel and a restaurant in what was the fabled Sky Terrace Room.

TULSA
BUILDING

"The KEY *to the* SUCCESS *of* PRESERVATION EFFORTS
LIES NOT *in the* ELIMINATION *of* DEMOLITION *and* URBAN RENEWAL,
but in a MERGING *of the* TWO *to* SHAPE
a FUTURE COMMUNITY *that* WILL GIVE US
the BEST *of the* OLD *and the* BEST *of the* NEW."

FROM PAGE ONE HUNDRED TWENTY

ENDURING PRESTIGE

MVNICIPAL BVILDING

FIFTY YEARS *of* SERVICE

DANIEL WEBSTER PATTON WAS elected as Tulsa's seventeenth mayor in April 1928, a mere three months after the opening of the Chamber's new Tulsa Building. He came into the job with a strong inclination for civic planning on a big scale. In fact, before he had even considered running for mayor, he had already deeply hewed a permanent legacy into the very earth of his city—a legacy that modern Tulsans still depend on every day. ¶ Dan had first come to Tulsa in 1901 as a sixteen-year-old apprentice to his older brother, Gus. Together they conducted Tulsa's first federal survey and the platting of the city. Despite working outside in a brutal 112-degree Oklahoma summer

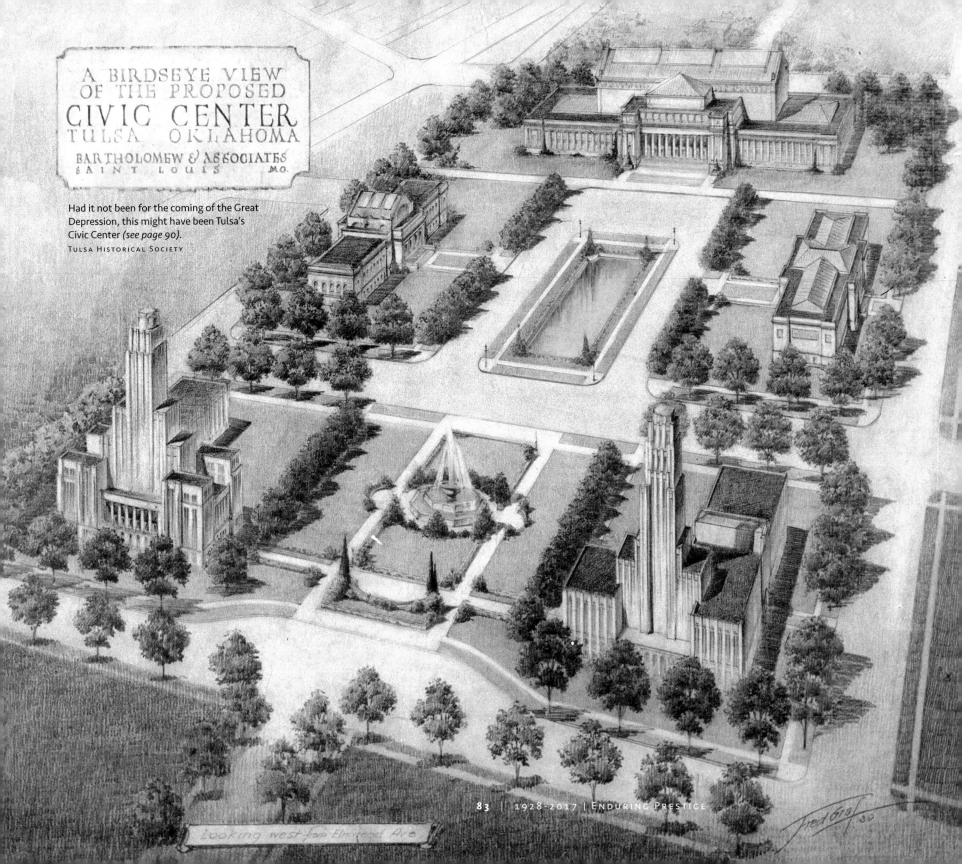

A BIRDSEYE VIEW
OF THE PROPOSED
CIVIC CENTER
TULSA OKLAHOMA
BARTHOLOMEW & ASSOCIATES
SAINT LOUIS MO.

Had it not been for the coming of the Great Depression, this might have been Tulsa's Civic Center *(see page 90)*.
TULSA HISTORICAL SOCIETY

Looking west from Elm Ave

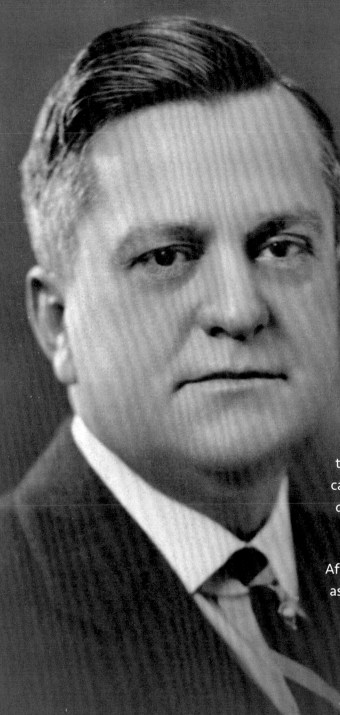

DANIEL W. PATTON

17*th* MAYOR *of* TULSA [1928-1930]

DAN PATTON CAME TO TULSA in 1901 from rural Arkansas, southwest of Fort Smith. An ambitious 15-year-old, he immediately made his mark on Tulsa while assisting his older brother, J. Gus Patton, in his survey work with the U.S. Department of the Interior. Together, they platted and surveyed Tulsa, a process that included establishing the street names still used today.

Engineering was in Dan's blood and his résumé quickly grew to include road and bridge work for both public needs and the railroads. Working in southwestern Oklahoma, Dan engineered for Le Flore and Pushmataha Counties, and served one term as the Mayor of Poteau before returning to Tulsa in 1917 to take a job as Tulsa County engineer, a position he would hold until 1926. In 1928, he caught a national wave of Republican victories and became Mayor of Tulsa. The wave didn't last long and he lost his re-election bid in 1930. After losing again in 1932, he gave up on politics and returned to engineering in his own private practice.

After World War II, Patton found himself working for the City of Tulsa again, this time as city engineer. It was in this role that he put forth the concept of a circular elevated highway system to provide badly needed access to downtown businesses. Patton's concept for the Inner Dispersal Loop was panned in the 1948 mayoral campaign by Democrat Roy B. Lundy who promised to "kill that silly expressway plan" if elected. Lundy won and, true to his word, fired Patton and killed the plan. Patton passed away in 1963, but not before seeing economic necessity revive his vision for the IDL.

TULSA HISTORICAL SOCIETY

Mayor Dan Patton, *seated second from the left in the front row,* poses with other city officials in his office in the Municipal Building, c.1928.

Mayor and Mrs. Dan Patton welcome popular vaudeville group, the Singer Midgets, to Tulsa on the front steps of the Municipal Building, 1930.

his first year in town, Patton fell in love with Tulsa. After a short absence spent engineering road systems in rural eastern Oklahoma, he eventually made Tulsa his home and solidified his professional credentials as the chief engineer for Tulsa County. Through his service both to the city and to the county, Patton helped to father not only the current layout and naming of Tulsa's city streets, but also Tulsa County's highway system and the interurban lines that became so vital in connecting Tulsa's workforce with its surrounding communities and oil fields. Considered Tulsa's first true civic planner, Dan Patton came into his term as mayor intent on bringing order to the compounding growing pains of Tulsa's infrastructure. He also intended to leave the office having given the city a plan for growth that would help avoid further problems in the future.

His first move in shaping that future was to retain the services of one of America's most progressive urban planners, Harland Bartholomew of Harland Bartholomew & Associates (HBA), St. Louis. Like Patton, Bartholomew

was a civil engineer by trade, whose passion for comprehensive urban planning grew, by necessity, out of his work on transportation plans. As a by-product of studying traffic flow, Bartholomew developed radical new solutions for urban design, zoning, and human interaction. In the summer of 1928, Bartholomew set about studying four specific areas of concern for Tulsa: transportation, zoning, parks and recreation, and the feasibility of Tulsa's first plan for addressing the need to expand its public buildings.

Four years earlier, under Mayor Newblock, the city had established the Tulsa Planning Commission and made its first serious attempt

Looking west on 4th Street from Cincinnati, 1929.
BERYL FORD COLLECTION

at a comprehensive development plan.[1] The product of that effort was the 1924 "Tulsa Plan," which conceptualized a dramatic European-style civic center anchored by a domed Union train depot and a towering five-hundred-foot monolith. Enclosing a central plaza, the plan envisioned a set of six Neoclassically designed city, county and federal buildings—one of which was, of course, a gigantic new City Hall. The only part of the plan that was even vaguely realized was the Union Depot, which opened in 1931. It is, however, interesting to note that the Tulsa Plan called for the demolition of six city blocks between Main and Cincinnati and Archer and 3rd, as well as placing the tallest feature of the skyline in perfect symmetry with a version of Boston Avenue that ended at 3rd Street—a nearly perfect foreshadowing of the Williams Center development that would come exactly fifty years later.

For his bite at Tulsa's development apple, Harland Bartholomew conducted an extensive study of the city's history, topography, demographics, growth trends, and tax base. He compiled his findings into a sweeping and brilliant assessment of the city's current needs, along with a coordinated list of solutions for dynamic long-term growth. In what came to be known as the Bartholomew Report, Tulsa received its most visionary comprehensive development plan to date. Along with a transportation study, a major street

The only part of the **1924 Tulsa Plan**'s vision for a unified civic center that was even vaguely realized was the **Union Depot**, which opened in 1931.
PUBLIC DOMAIN

The Tulsa Plan's Civic Center, 1924.

Bordered by the railroad tracks to the north, 2nd Street on the south, Main Street on the west and Cincinnati Avenue on the east, the 1924 Tulsa Plan's vision for a civic center included *(clockwise from lower left)* a federal building, county courthouse, public library, union depot, municipal auditorium, municipal building, and a hall of records. These seven structures were to be built around a vast central plaza anchored by a 500-foot monolith that placed the tallest feature of the skyline in perfect symmetry with a version of Boston Avenue that ended at 3rd Street—a nearly perfect foreshadowing of the Williams Center development that would come exactly fifty years later. TULSA HISTORICAL SOCIETY

The Bartholomew Plan's Civic Center, 1930.

According to Bartholomew's May 21, 1930, letter of transmittal, "In this report the relative merits of eight locations [for a civic center] were analyzed and discussed, and the site selected is the only one that satisfactorily meets all the requirements." Locating the Civic Center on the west side of downtown was one of the few lasting legacies of Bartholomew's efforts. The previously debated question of location was one of the few general similarities of the many subsequent plans. When the Architectural League of Tulsa's plan was finally accepted in 1955, the site had only moved one block south and west to include the already standing Tulsa County Courthouse.

The stunning contrast between **Bartholomew's civic center concept** and the first modernist vision presented by Murray McCune only 14 years later *(see page 103)* is indicative of how radically World War II changed America's view of futurism and how quickly the Mid-Century Modern movement captured the public's fancy. *Left:* Bartholomew's civic center looking east down 4th Street toward downtown with his vision for a new Convention Hall in the foreground. *Below:* Bartholomew's concept for replacing the Municipal Building— interesting when compared with the final City Hall Tower completed in 1969. Tulsa Historical Society

HOUSTON AVE.

Looking East from Houston Ave.

plan, and recommended alterations to Tulsa's rudimentary zoning ordinances, Bartholomew also agreed with the 1924 Tulsa Plan's view of grouping replacements for virtually every downtown public building into a common location—although it was nowhere near the railroads, which, in Bartholomew's view, complicated access and created noise problems.

Suggesting instead a site on the west side of downtown between 3rd and 5th Streets and Elwood and Houston, he also recommended that the design of the structures be in keeping with Tulsa's

Harland Bartholomew

Born in Stoneham, Massachusetts, in 1889, Harland Bartholomew moved to New York City when he was 15 and attended Erasmus Hall High School in Brooklyn. After two years studying civil engineering at Rutgers University, Bartholomew left school due to a lack of money. Naturally skillful, he found work that exposed him to the concepts of city planning. Bartholomew's visionary solutions to meet challenges brought by the rise of the automobile eventually made him North America's preeminent pioneer of modern urban planning. In addition to his work for Tulsa, he produced plans for major American and Canadian cities from Los Angeles to Washington, D.C.

already impressive—and still rapidly expanding—collection of Art Deco, Beaux-Arts, and neo-Gothic monuments. "Public buildings represent the dignity and importance of a city," he wrote. "They should be outstanding buildings, both in themselves and in their settings. To be seen and appreciated, they should be located at the focal positions and set off by adequate and appropriate open spaces."[2]

To illustrate this concept, he provided a fantastic conceptual rendering showing a new city hall and a new county courthouse in the form of two juxtaposed, modernistic twenty-story Art Deco skyscrapers set back into green spaces that fronted a dignified six-square-block configuration. Behind the two towers and around a central park stood three elegant Neoclassical structures, built to house a combined art museum and Indian memorial, a public library, and a massive new assembly center to replace the current Convention Hall (known today as the Brady Theater).

The Bartholomew Report was breathtaking—both in the loftiness of its vision and its price tag. Patton and his commissioners had anticipated the cost, but when they engaged HBA in the summer of 1928, money seemed to be the least of Tulsa's concerns. Every successive year of the Roaring Twenties had brought bigger and better things to the

Magic City. The city was flying high, with no end in sight. The four-hundred-foot tower of the Exchange National Bank Building (known today as the 320 South Boston Building) had just been completed, Tulsa was hosting its most successful International Petroleum Expo to date, and, as if to top it all off, the city had just received national attention after the United States Navy's seven-hundred-foot Zeppelin, the u.s.s. *Los Angeles*, saluted the Oil Capital of the World by flying laps around downtown. By the time the Bartholomew Report was delivered, however, everything had changed.

At the end of October 1929, just as HBA was drawing its final conclusions for Tulsa's grand development proposal, the stock market in New York City crashed, marking the

onset of the Great Depression that would consume the nation for the next decade. On May 21, 1930, while the entire world was struggling to come to terms with the new realities of economic uncertainty, Harland Bartholomew presented the last of his four reports—his civic center plan.

Despite this most unfortunate coincident timing, the Bartholomew Report was not an immediate casualty of the looming Great Depression. Surprisingly, neither was a far-reaching $6.8 million infrastructure bond package that Mayor Patton had spent most of 1929 masterminding to meet maintenance needs and selected infrastructure recommendations from Bartholomew's street and zoning plans. Although Patton's bond package passed muster with the voters, he did not. In April 1930, Mayor Patton was defeated by his Democratic opponent, Tulsa's eighteenth mayor, George L. Watkins. Still, Patton could leave City Hall with his head held high, having given Tulsa much

The *U.S.S. Los Angeles* salutes the Oil Capital of the World with an honorary flyby on October 9, 1928, symbolically marking the high-water mark of Tulsa's oil-boom era.
BERYL FORD COLLECTION

The ONSET *of the* GREAT DEPRESSION AWARDED *the* MUNICIPAL BUILDING *a* SECOND LEASE *on* LIFE. *In* RETURN, TULSA'S DILIGENT LITTLE CITY HALL SET ABOUT *its* INTENDED PURPOSE *as the* NOBLE WORKHORSE *of* CITY GOVERNMENT.

of what it needed immediately as well as an optimistic view of its future self. Although it was not appreciated in time to impress the voters, his infrastructure levy planted the seeds for more public works projects than had any prior administration[3]—a fact that became extremely important in very short order.

For most of 1930, the strength of Tulsa's oil economy provided cautious optimism that the nation's economic woes might pass by the Magic City. Regrettably, that optimism did not last long. The realities of the Depression finally arrived with the onset of winter. By the dawn of 1931, Tulsa's economy

had collapsed—and with it, the inspiring vision for Tulsa's Civic Center contained within the Bartholomew Report.

Although initially doomed to the proverbial ash heap of history by the unmanageable speed of the Magic City's growth, the onset of the Great Depression awarded the Municipal Building a second lease on life. In return, Tulsa's diligent little City Hall set about its intended purpose as the noble workhorse of city government. All told, the building would go on to dutifully fulfill that role for a total of fifty years—nearly every day of which was marked by complaints of overcrowded halls and cramped offices. But with the focus of city government having shifted from a mind-set of growing Tulsa's splendor to merely sustaining its people, the sentiments from that *Morning Tulsa Daily World* editorial written about the city's quest for a better city hall back on April 17, 1915, rang true once again: "Many would prefer, from reasons of civic pride, to see a new City Hall built … but it is urged that economic reasons make it necessary to be content with what is available, rather than what is desirable."[4]

Mohawk Park construction, 1934. During Mayor Herman Newblock's second stint in office (1932-1934), twenty-seven Works Progress Administration (WPA) projects, including the Mohawk Park Lake, put Depression-struck Tulsans to work. The Tulsa Rose Garden, Tracy Park tennis courts, and clearing the Bird Creek channel were among other WPA projects. BERYL FORD COLLECTION

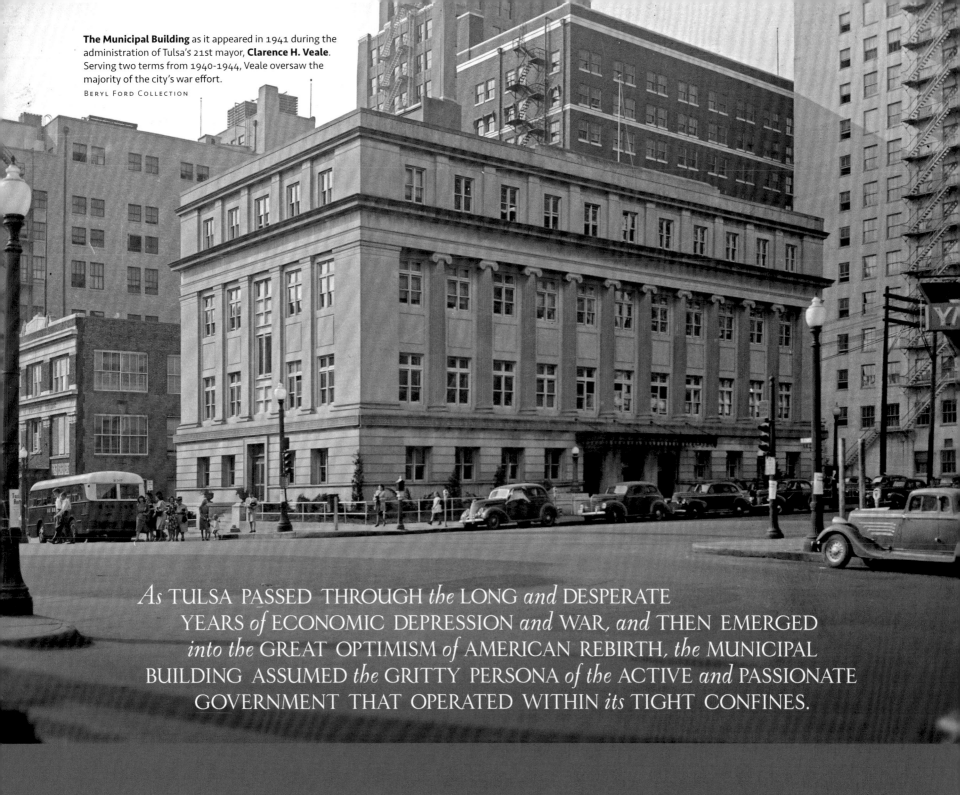

The Municipal Building as it appeared in 1941 during the administration of Tulsa's 21st mayor, **Clarence H. Veale**. Serving two terms from 1940-1944, Veale oversaw the majority of the city's war effort.

BERYL FORD COLLECTION

As TULSA PASSED THROUGH *the* LONG *and* DESPERATE
YEARS *of* ECONOMIC DEPRESSION *and* WAR, *and* THEN EMERGED
into the GREAT OPTIMISM *of* AMERICAN REBIRTH, *the* MUNICIPAL
BUILDING ASSUMED *the* GRITTY PERSONA *of the* ACTIVE *and* PASSIONATE
GOVERNMENT THAT OPERATED WITHIN *its* TIGHT CONFINES.

As Tulsa passed through the long and desperate years of economic depression and war, and then emerged into the great optimism of American rebirth, the Municipal Building assumed the gritty persona of the active and passionate government that operated within its tight confines. The raised voices and boiling passions of political discord filled its chambers throughout the course of seventeen administrations, eight Republican and nine Democrat. Through its halls, decades of disgruntled traffic violators and utility customers dragged defeated steps across sullied enameled bricks as they reluctantly surrendered fines, fees, and payments through the first-floor teller windows. Decades of cigarette, pipe, and cigar smoke eventually dulled the noble visages that looked down from the mural hanging above the 4th Street lobby upon jostling crowds of harried citizens, barristers, and officials from every walk of life. Protesters fighting for one cause or another marched their slow circuits past the rain- and dust-streaked front steps, where bedraggled men cradling bottles in crumpled brown bags watched with little curiosity. Above the constant bustle of Tulsa's busy streets, multimillion-dollar favors were called in behind heavy oak doors locked tightly against the prying eyes of curious reporters and suspicious rivals. By day, the never-ending business of variances and valuations, economic initiatives and legislative agendas, plodded on under the public view of conscientious members of the press. After hours, those same issues were settled out of the public eye in colorful language over bootlegged whiskey and thick cigars. And then there were the budgets—always the budgets: who would win, who would lose, and who would *really* settle the bills for Tulsa's never-ending progress. Such was the Municipal Building's long and rigorous life as Tulsa's seat of power.

Throughout the decades, the relationship between the Municipal Building and those who occupied it or frequented it wavered from familial comfort to open disdain. The feelings of most likely moved between those two extremes from day to day, depending on the adequacy of the window-mounted air conditioners and the famously cantankerous mood of the single elevator. In 1958, while writing for the *Tulsa Tribune*, Frosty Troy reported on the overcrowded and declining state of the building: "'The sooner it falls down, the sooner a new building will rise,' is the philosophy of the many at City Hall,"

he wrote. "They say the building is worth more 'dead' than 'alive.'"[5] While Troy's report no doubt captured the feeling of "the many" quite accurately, it was not an opinion shared by everyone.

Former Tulsa District Attorney, S.M. "Buddy" Fallis, who was starting his legal career during that same period, came away with a very different impression. His first memories of the Municipal Building were from the early 1950s, when, as a teenager, he fell in love with the building while

Gallery of Mayors. A familiar feature on the Municipal Building's third floor was an every-growing portrait gallery showing each of Tulsa's mayors. A close examination of the photo below shows it was taken in the late 1940s—the latest mayor in the gallery being Lee Price Jr., who served from 1946-1948. These original portraits didn't make the trip to the City Hall Tower in 1969 and today reside in the archives of the Tulsa Historical Society.
BERYL FORD COLLECTION

The Busy Life of the People's House.

The city's business, the ceremonial photos, and city commission meetings were all part of the day-to-day activities in Tulsa's busy City Hall. Photos from the L.C. Clark Collection at the Tulsa Historical Society provide a glimpse into the commonplace as well as the poised during the mid-1950s. Clark, a retired hardware store owner, defeated Attorney John W. McCune to serve as Tulsa's 27th mayor from 1954 to 1956. Also elected in 1954 was Elizabeth Stowell Anderson *(lower left photo, and far right center photo)*, Tulsa's second female city auditor. The first was J.D. Seaman whose signature (signed as "Mrs. Frank Seaman") approved the Spavinaw Water Project Bond in 1921 *(see page 77)*.

ALL IMAGES: TULSA HISTORICAL SOCIETY

Mayor Clark with **Commissioner Sid Patterson** and **City Auditor Elizabeth Anderson**.

Mrs. Helen Orson, daughter **Nancy**, son **David** of Neenah, Wisconsin, receiving an honorary police escort from City Hall to McClure Swimming Pool on July 26, 1955.

Mayor L.C. Clark's administrative council poses for a photo in the Commission Meeting Hall during the 1955 City Hall Christmas party.

Sgt. Bill Harp with the Tulsa Police Department speaking during a city commission meeting, 1955.

City Auditor Elizabeth Anderson addresses citizens during a city commission meeting, 1955.

Citizen participants during a city commission meeting.

City Hall's Biggest Night.

Having missed her opportunity for a celebratory grand opening in 1919, the Municipal Building's big gala would come 35 years later when Mayor L.C. Clark made City Hall the center of what likely still holds the record as the biggest celebration of Tulsa's government. Beginning the evening of November 4, 1954, Clark kicked off the four-day Municipal Parade & Open House with an enormous street parade that started with Tulsa's Shrine Band, featured floats from every city department, and required two hours to pass the review stand on the front steps of City Hall. The event, intended to "acquaint Tulsans with the operations and functions of their government," included dozens of educational displays that explained the inner workings of the city. As special

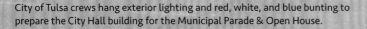

City of Tulsa crews hang exterior lighting and red, white, and blue bunting to prepare the City Hall building for the Municipal Parade & Open House.

hostesses walked tours through City Hall, those waiting their turn were regaled by the slow procession of every imaginable piece of machinery behind city maintenance followed by marching formations of 40 policemen, 50 firemen, 100 members of the Junior Police Corps, and the Central High Marching Band. The evening concluded with a performance from the "City Hall Trio" and a massive square dance that filled 4th Street between Boston and Cincinnati.

97

"I'D LOOK OVER *at this* BUILDING *and* THINK HOW PRETTY IT WAS—*and it is a* BEAUTIFUL BUILDING. THEN YOU THINK ABOUT IT, *that it is* WORN; *it has* DONE *its* DUTY. THEY EVEN TALKED ABOUT TEARING *it* DOWN..."

visiting the YMCA directly across 4th Street. "Lot of times while waiting on the bus, I'd look over at this building and think how pretty it was—and it is a beautiful building. Just looking at it, it was very impressive to me, rightfully so. Then you think about it, that it is worn; it has done its duty. They even talked about tearing it down. But luckily someone had some sense about it and started to preserve our historical values rather than take it like you would a bad tooth."[6]

Regardless of anyone's feeling about the old building, Tulsa would have to make do until a

Municipal Building Memories—Tom Birmingham, City Hall reporter and city legal department attorney who later went into private practice, looks over a photo of the old city commission meeting room *(top left, page 95)* and notes that it not only looks small but was small. "There's the rail that separated the public from the commissioners. I remember the press sat back here, and I remember there was a city commission zoning hearing and this poor devil got up and he was protesting whatever the zoning was and he was standing at the podium in front of everybody. He started turning blue and turning purple and he just dropped stone dead right on the floor. Lou Levy in the legal department jumped over [the rail] and started working on him and of course they called the paramedics, but he was dead as a door nail. I remember that ... not only did people work there, they died there."

replacement could be worked out. Even though the city had outgrown many of the problems that had complicated and delayed the construction of the Municipal Building, the process of replacing it came with an entirely new set of problems, the most significant being the grand vision of a civic center.

IN HIS 1929 report, Harland Bartholomew famously warned, "A civic center that is well-located, adequate in size, and outstanding in design is an asset which increases in value as the years pass. A cheap compromise will soon become a matter of deep regret."[7] Consequently, a replacement for the Municipal Building would never be as simple as just building a bigger city hall. In the mind of city planners, City Hall had to be a part of a grand civic center. The economic realities of the 1930s made it impossible to consider development plans so grand. But every subsequent decade would see lofty proposals for a civic center that would forever change the face of Tulsa.

In 1943, a combined city/county post-war planning commission headed by local businessman Glen Ames published its proposal for a grandiose civic center to be built around a twenty-four-floor tower rising above a 7,500-seat civic auditorium. Filling the two city blocks between Denver and Boulder and 3rd and 4th, the tower and the auditorium was to form a tunnel through which Cheyenne could run unimpeded. Stating with confidence that their solution would be sufficient to meet the city's needs for the next hundred years, the plan also recommended the construction of a secondary airport near downtown. The imaginative proposal was impressively illustrated by a highly accomplished and well-regarded *Tulsa World* staff artist named Clarence Allen. In addition to a city hall and a county courthouse, Allen's schematic also featured an enormous terrazzo plaza with a memorial for the still-ongoing war, as well as accommodations for a parking garage (then called "automobile storage") and a landing pad for helicopter traffic to and from the airport.

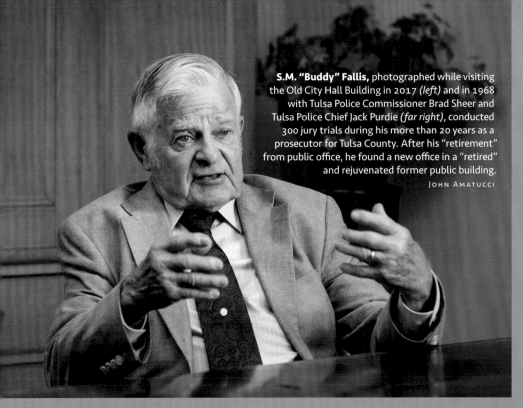

S.M. "Buddy" Fallis, photographed while visiting the Old City Hall Building in 2017 (left) and in 1968 with Tulsa Police Commissioner Brad Sheer and Tulsa Police Chief Jack Purdie (far right), conducted 300 jury trials during his more than 20 years as a prosecutor for Tulsa County. After his "retirement" from public office, he found a new office in a "retired" and rejuvenated former public building.
JOHN AMATUCCI

TULSA TRIBUNE

"The Building Can't Get Rid of Me!"

Reflections on seventy years of admiration from the Municipal Building's longest-residing tenant, Attorney S.M. "Buddy" Fallis.

He would stand on the south side of the YMCA building across the street from Tulsa's Municipal Building. A self-described youngster from "the wrong side of the tracks" waiting for the bus to take him home. It was the Depression, and, if "you paid a certain amount, you could come down once a month ... and you could even swim in the pool and all," he recalls.

Decades later, after seeing his name in numerous headlines as Tulsa's district attorney, S.M. "Buddy" Fallis would spend several decades with the address of the building he admired as a youngster on his business card.

His connection grew from youthful admiration to city employee when, in junior high school, he landed the groundskeeper job at Archer Park. "I would come down to City Hall and pick up my check once a month at the cage on the west side of the lobby."

The groundskeeper would go on to attend The University of Tulsa, clerk in the County Courthouse, earn his law degree, join the county attorney's office, and be elected district attorney. After some 20 years of public service, he recalls, "I got a position with Nichols, Wolfe [law firm] and that brought me back to the place [Old City Hall] where it all started."

In 1994, as he contemplated retirement, he was convinced to join Fred Dorwart's law firm, which had moved into Old City Hall. "So I returned to the building again. The building can't get rid of me. Yes, in the same office. Didn't have to change the furniture out."

These many years later, Buddy Fallis reflects on the building he spent more time in than any other. "They even talked about tearing it down. But luckily someone had some sense about it and started to preserve our historical values rather than take it out like a bad tooth. And then the architects got together and saved it. Gave it life, both life inside of it and life outside of it. I love history, and it has a strong heartbeat today because of the work these people did."

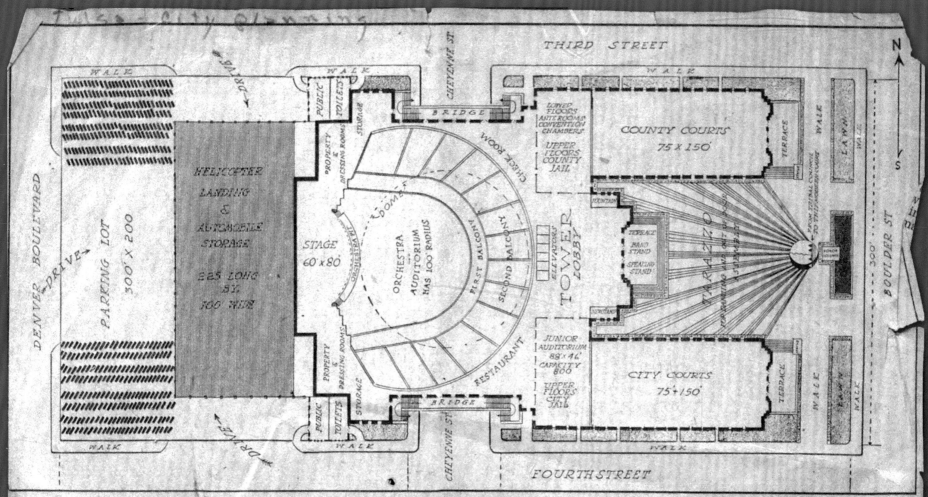

Visualization by Clarence Canning Allen

DANCING, TOO—Almost every city-county activity could be accommodated in the city-county-civic center proposed by the post-war planning commission. Floor plan indicates the entrance on Boulder avenue, with city offices on one side, county offices on the other. Additional office space would be in a 24-story tower. At center is a huge auditorium which would seat from 5,000 to 7,000 persons. At rear is a helicopter landing area and auto storage facilities.

The Post-War Planning Commission's Civic Center, 1943.

Upon publishing the concept for a 24-story skyscraper and a one-square-mile secondary airport closer to downtown, the *Tulsa Tribune* rightly observed, "Whether [city] commissioners will approve the proposal or order architect's plans drawn, or whether they will 'receive and file' the idea for drawing plans at a later date, was problematical." And as supposed, the concept was never approved to move forward. However, the war-time vision for Tulsa's Civic Center was an inspiring indication that years of depression and worldwide conflict did not smother the community's vision of Tulsa's creative grandeur. TULSA TRIBUNE

Although nothing apparently became of the 1943 plan, it did serve the vital role of keeping Tulsa's longing for a grand civic center alive and well. In 1950, the Chamber of Commerce began a new push that resulted in the formation of a dynamic and forward-thinking professional group that tackled the civic center problem by forming a nonprofit organization they called the Architectural League of Tulsa. Sitting at the head of the table was one of Tulsa's most accomplished and visionary architects of the mid-century modern movement, Murray McCune of his Tulsa-based firm, McCune-Jones-McCune.[8]

"To spur a little imagination on the subject," McCune published a conceptual rendering of a civic center in August 1954.[9] McCune's plan occupied roughly the same pottage recommended by the Bartholomew Report in 1929, but shifted it a block farther south to include the northwest corner of 6th & Boulder, where Tulsa County was just finishing the construction of a new courthouse. More than simply spurring a little imagination, his rendering became the basis for what would ultimately become Tulsa's Civic Center.

Along with the Chamber of Commerce, Tulsa's twenty-seventh mayor, L.C. Clark, eagerly embraced the work of McCune and the Architectural League. "Our present City Hall quarters are sadly outmoded and not in keeping with the position Tulsa occupies as a metropolitan city,"[10] Mayor Clark was quoted as saying. "It is the unanimous feeling of the city commission that a new city hall should be provided."[11]

Mayor Clark had been around Tulsa long enough to remember when the Municipal Building was new and welcomed. But, he quickly pointed out, "[that] was built back when Tulsa had a population of about 70,000."[12] By the mid-1950s, Tulsa had grown to over 200,000 citizens. Even with the entire building—including the once-grand fourth-floor auditorium—cut up into cubbyhole offices to accommodate as many city employees as possible, most of the non-executive or legal functions of government had already migrated out of the building. Parks and Recreation, the Metropolitan Planning Commission, and Traffic Engineering had moved to what was known as the City Hall Annex four blocks west, at 406 South Denver, where the Tulsa City-County Library now stands. The utilities and refuse departments had

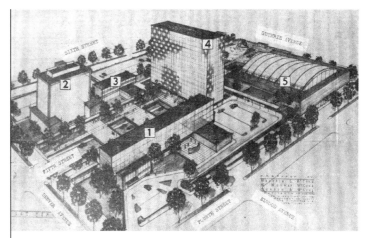

"To spur a little imagination on the subject," McCune published this conceptual rendering of a modern civic center in August 1954. It was the first expression of a modernist view of Tulsa's Civic Center dream. TULSA TRIBUNE

landed in other commercial office space located in a now-demolished building at the corner of 6th & Cincinnati. The Water and Sewer Departments eventually wound up on the west side of the river at 23rd & Jackson.[13]

With the promise of a unified Tulsa government functioning comfortably inside one single, modern tower, Mayor Clark and the city commission accepted the League's vision with great enthusiasm. Thus began two decades of popular modernism, which promised the Tulsa of tomorrow a radical new design and the glory of international attention. While it was, indeed, all of those things, the same crusade that built the Civic Center would also result in wide swaths of downtown being reduced to asphalt parking lots, the second destruction of the Greenwood District, and the demolition of the majority of Tulsa's oil-boom architecture.

LOVE *an* OLD BUILDING

I N HARLAND BARTHOLOMEW'S VIEW, one of the keys to raising successful public buildings was to ensure that the design was in keeping with the preexisting architecture of the city it represented. But America came back from World War II craving a very different self-image than had the industrial titans who built elegant castles as evidence of their own hard-won achievements. The popular new mid-century modern movement called, instead, for a radical departure from the preexisting world order of traditional expressions of power, wealth, and prestige. Modernism was not intended to pair nicely with traditionalism. It intended to unseat it. Thus was the intention behind the bold new

City Hall Tower

200 Civic Center. Having garnered international attention for its brilliant, modernist design, City Hall Tower was the last jewel of the vaunted Civic Center to fall into place. Before the Civic Center's tenth birthday, however, articles regarding maintenance and engineering complications had become familiar topics to local reporters.
TULSA HISTORICAL SOCIETY

vision for Tulsa's Civic Center propagated by the Architectural League of Tulsa.

As explained in the Civic Center's 2012 application for the National Register of Historic Places, "the architecture was chosen to represent the visual essence of 'government' in Tulsa after World War II. Tulsa, like many cities after the end of the war, wanted to look toward a bright new future, and turned its view toward an architecture that could convey that the city was in step with a post-World War II modern world. As an Architectural League report noted, 'A unified Civic Center would be a symbol of Tulsa's progressive spirit.'"[1]

Donald McCormick, FAIA (left) presents the Architectural League of Tulsa's Civic Center plan to **Mayor L.C. Clark** in 1955.

In the process of developing the Civic Center, the League worked around two major designs, the original model from 1955 and a second major revision made in 1959. The final product looked very little like either, but it still fit the bill for "radical departure." As promised, the League's designs attracted international attention and approval in award competitions, publications, studies, and opinions. Founding secretary-general of the Congrès International d'Architecture Moderne, professor of architecture at MIT and Harvard, and respected architecture critic, Sigfried Giedion, recognized the early design of the Civic Center as one of the most significant examples of architecture for community planning in the last century.[2]

Giedion passed away before Tulsa completed its civic center. It would have been interesting to read his opinion of how the dramatic futurist philosophizing of the League evolved when confronted with the realities of engineering, construction, and, of course, budget. Tulsans overwhelmingly preferred the idealism of the models to the toned-down practicality of the finished product. Regardless, the 1969 opening of City Hall Tower brought to fulfillment the grand civic-center dream for which every Tulsa mayor and every city planner had longed for each of the forty-five years since the Municipal Building had been deemed inadequate.

In what seemed only fitting, given Tulsa's chronic history of delayed gratification for suitable city halls, the new City Hall Tower, designed principally by McCune himself, was the last piece added to the Civic Center complex. It arrived a fashionable five years late and significantly over budget. And in yet another undeniably ironic coincident of fate, Tulsa's twenty-ninth mayor, James Maxwell, who had shepherded the Civic Center's development throughout his entire eight-year term, befell the same fate as Mayor Simmons. Maxwell, the city's youngest and most charismatic executive, the perfect man to lead the Oil Capital's charge into modernism, was, like Simmons, denied by Tulsa's electorate the honor of occupying his new City Hall. In March 1969—exactly fifty years to the month since Mayor Hubbard had transferred City Hall governance from the Reeder Building to Simmons's Municipal Building—Tulsa's thirtieth mayor, James M. Hewgley Jr., officially transferred Tulsa's seat of power from the Municipal Building into Maxwell's City Hall Tower.

IRONICALLY, EXACTLY 50 YEARS AFTER MAYOR SIMMONS *was* DENIED *the* HONOR *of* OCCUPYING HIS NEW CITY HALL, *the* SAME FATE BEFELL MAYOR MAXWELL.

Although bearing little resemblance to the final product, **the 1955 model for the Tulsa Civic Center** received international praise from architecture critic Sigfried Giedion who recognized it as one of the most significant examples of architecture for community planning in the last century.
TULSA FOUNDATION FOR ARCHITECTURE ARCHIVE

JAMES L. MAXWELL
29th MAYOR *of* TULSA [1958-1966]

WHETHER IT WAS HIS YOUTH (elected mayor at the age of 31) or dedication, James L. Maxwell earned a reputation as a tireless worker. He came by this honestly—regularly rising at 4:00 a.m. to be at his Municipal Building desk by 6:00 a.m. Some evenings he would attend as many as five functions, often necessitating up to three changes in clothes. He said that if people wanted their mayor to be somewhere he should be there.

Maxwell's often 16-hour days were not for show—during his four consecutive terms he pushed for a downtown civic center, for a nationally recognized downtown central library, for an expanded and improved expressway system, for the relocation of the city's airport, for the purchase of the Gilcrease Museum, and for the integration of public accommodations.

A 1944 Tulsa Central High School graduate, Maxwell enlisted in the Army and served combat duty in India, Burma and China. He returned and graduated from Oklahoma A&M (now Oklahoma State University) where he was president of the Student Senate. After his tenure as mayor ended, Maxwell worked as a consultant in Washington, D.C., managed the family's downtown flower shop, and, at the time of his death in 1984, had returned to public service as program director for the Oklahoma Corporation Commission.

TULSA HISTORICAL SOCIETY

It's Maxwell Time

The city's most popular and youngest mayor ushered Tulsa into a new era.

Tulsa's second longest-serving and youngest mayor led the effort that resulted in the abandonment of the City Hall he first presided over when elected in 1958. That is one of the two most significant events of his term, which ended in 1966. One lasting: the creation of Tulsa's Civic Center (and a new City Hall in 1969). The other equally significant for its time: the advancement of civil rights in the early 1960s, without the anguish and agitation noted in other U.S. cities at the time.

Two long-time city-hall insiders—Charles Norman, who served as city attorney for nine years, and Tom Birmingham, who covered City Hall for the *Tulsa Tribune* and later worked in the city's legal department—both point to James Maxwell's leadership in advancing both causes.

Elected after what historians call a "friendly" campaign, James Maxwell was a thirty-one-year-old flower shop owner. Long-time Tulsa radio and television reporter and anchor Clayton Vaughn recalls that Maxwell's victory signaled the emergence of young businessmen, primarily local Jaycees (officially known then as the Junior Chamber of Commerce), into the political arena. "The Maxwell election symbolized the end of an era and the beginning of a new one for Tulsans."

As Maxwell assumed office, the long-ignored issue of civil rights began to come to the forefront. Charles Norman recalls (in a 2008 interview with Vaughn) that the city's

legal department was asked to determine if the municipal government had the authority to adopt an ordinance concerning public accommodations. The conclusion was that, under the need to promote the "general welfare," the city commission had such power.

But how was Tulsa, with its deep Southern Democratic roots, able to easily adopt such an ordinance, one of the first in the nation?

"It was implemented through Jim Maxwell's leadership with very, very little conflict or objection," recalled Norman. "Jim Maxwell went to the black leadership, who in many cases were ministers of the churches in North Tulsa, and told them he was going to integrate the restaurants in Tulsa—lunch counters, cafeterias and whatever—and I [Maxwell] need your cooperation for all to not go to the same place on the same day."

It was a call for gradualism that worked.

Then there was City Hall itself. Studies, proposals, and dreams had come and gone. In his book, *Tulsa! Biography of the American City,* Danney Goble sums up the Maxwell touch: "In his first year as mayor, Maxwell persuaded the public to approve $7.2 million in bonds to build a new civic center. Over the next five years, he got another $24 million to construct an entire complex that covered twelve city blocks and provided modernized, architecturally integrated city and county office buildings."

Mayor Maxwell helped make that dream become a reality. And left more than one indelible mark on his city.

The TRANSFER of City Hall left the old Municipal Building's future very much in doubt. With no prospect for it beyond liquidation for the value of its land, city workers boarded up the tired and worn old building, leaving it in a terrible state, with trash and debris littering hallways and stairs. After appraisers devalued the real estate based on the presence of the building, the City Commission published an offer to accept sealed bids for the property.[3] Surprisingly, they received no offers. But, given the development trend sweeping the city at the time, any bid offered at that point would have been a death sentence for the building.

Tulsa was in the grip of a nearly hysterical teardown craze that would ultimately result in the demolition of nearly 80 percent of the city's central business district—most of it falling in a busy ten-year window between 1965 and 1975.[4] Both private and government development, spurred on by the federal Urban Renewal initiative, were bulldozing entire neighborhoods, leveling full city blocks, and dynamiting Tulsa's oil boom monuments as quickly as contractors could move from one project to the next. The Municipal Building sat right

The Municipal Building as it entered its final decade as City Hall. This picture was taken during the administration of Mayor James Maxwell, c.1960.
TULSA HISTORICAL SOCIETY

The TRANSFER *of* CITY HALL LEFT *the* OLD MUNICIPAL BUILDING'S FUTURE VERY MUCH *in* DOUBT.

Movers transferred the city's offices from the old Municipal Building to the new City Hall Tower in the Civic Center during the weekend of May 16-18, 1969.
TULSA WORLD

Pickets protest Urban Renewal. Five pickets, led by Leon Gilmore *(hatless, in the foreground)* parade in front of the Municipal Building to protest a proposed Urban Renewal project. Gilmore's sign, turned away from the camera, read "Stop Creeping Socialism. Urban Renewal Violates the Principles of Free Enterprise."

in the crosshairs of this trend, not merely because of its classification as an outmoded building, but primarily because of its potentially valuable location.

Having received no immediate interest in the property, the City Commission approved a negotiated sale on the open market.[5] In 1971, the Tulsa Community Chest, forerunner of today's Tulsa Area United Way, approached Tulsa's thirty-first mayor, Bob LaFortune, elected in 1970 when Hewgley chose not to seek a third term, with an offer to lease the Municipal Building for use as their headquarters. "I would be receptive to such a proposition," said Mayor LaFortune. "It would appear that the other alternative is a parking lot."[6] The deal failed to materialize and, as predicted by LaFortune,

This is
Tulsa
THE OIL CAPITAL OF THE WORLD

America's
Most
Beautiful
City

Architect's rendering of the final design for the Civic Center Plaza. The Federal Housing Acts of 1949 and 1954 financially incentivized private businesses to demolish full blocks of older inner-city construction for modernization and reuse. On the west side of downtown Tulsa, the city, county, state, and federal governments led by example when they razed more than fourteen city blocks to build Tulsa's new Civic Center and other modern government buildings.
BERYL FORD COLLECTION

the next offer came from a developer with eyes set solidly on demolition.

In July 1972, The Dorchester Company, the real-estate valuation and investment company at the center of much of Tulsa's Urban Renewal activity, put five hundred dollars down on an option to purchase the Municipal Building for the value of its

lot. When the news of the potential purchase broke, the *Tulsa Tribune* asked Don Dorchester Jr. about his intentions, should his offer be accepted. While expressing his regrets, he confirmed his company's intention to level the building.

"We've done a lot of soul-searching on this question of historic preservation," Dorchester allowed. "We wish the old building weren't located where it is. If it were a block or two east, it could be preserved." Explaining that, in their view, the value of 4th & Cincinnati was too significant not to develop further, he assured the *Tribune* that their efforts would lead to "something we think is especially significant for Tulsa."[7]

Being experts in commercial real estate, The Dorchester Company was undoubtedly accurate in their view of the Municipal Building. From the perspective of straight economics, the Municipal Building had significant limitations. It wasn't nearly large enough to fully exploit the value of its location, and, while it was a beautiful building, it was not exceptionally

From the PERSPECTIVE *of* STRAIGHT ECONOMICS, *the* MUNICIPAL BUILDING *had* SIGNIFICANT LIMITATIONS.

Municipal Building Memories—One of the partners in the law firm that participated in the original purchase of Old City Hall, recalled his first encounter: "One of my vivid memories is walking in there—I had been in the construction business—and it looked like a bomb had gone off. They had stripped those walls down to the concrete. So when they asked if there was any asbestos, I said that I know there is not any of that because there wasn't *anything* left."

distinctive for its architectural genre. Whatever intrinsic value it had was impossible to prove by number-crunching alone.

At some point, while the Municipal Building sat empty and shuttered with seemingly no hope for preservation, an unknown passerby painted the words *"Love an Old Building"* on one of the rough plywood panels hammered over the front doors. Whether the message was intended as a protest or an entreaty, it reflected the feelings of many Tulsans who were upset by the mass execution of so many of the buildings and neighborhoods with which they had grown up. The comfort of the familiar is a powerful element in the cohesiveness of any community. And perhaps no building was more familiar

to the citizenry than the Old City Hall they had grown up knowing so intimately through fifty years of personal interactions and through daily local news reports. In fact, longtime KOTV newsman Clayton Vaughn, who had covered City Hall most of his career, speculated that, had it not been for the words "MUNICIPAL BUILDING" carved across the top of its ten Ionic columns to remind the community of all the history that had occurred within its walls, it might not have survived Urban Renewal.[8]

Whether it was those letters, placed there fifty-five years earlier by Rush, Endacott & Rush, or the hand-painted sentiment scribbled that year by some unknown street philosopher, there were at least two men in Tulsa who took

IMAGES ON PAGES 111-114

After Coleman and Ervin acquired the Municipal Building in September 1972, the first order of business was to evaluate the condition of their new purchase. These survey photos capture the shocking state of the building after it sat vacant for three years following the transfer of City Hall to the Civic Center. Vandals, vagrants, and pigeons left their mark—and their odor—on the building, adding to the decay from 50 years of hard public use.

Captured in the center two photos above, architect **Jay Sparks**, a young member of the Coleman, Ervin & Associates team at the time, stands in to help measure scale. By the end of the project, Sparks had moved on to an exceptional career managing his own firm, Sparks Design, in St. Louis, Missouri.

OLD CITY HALL BUILDING ARCHIVE

Had the WORDS "MUNICIPAL BUILDING" NOT BEEN THERE *to* REMIND *the* COMMUNITY *of all the* HISTORY *that had* OCCURRED WITHIN *its* WALLS, *it* MIGHT NOT *have* SURVIVED URBAN RENEWAL.

notice and placed enough value on the Municipal Building's history to take a risk on saving it. More than just an expression of love for an old building, their decision became a turning point in downtown Tulsa's development, with reverberations that would reach far beyond the Municipal Building and forever change the way Tulsa's architectural heritage would be evaluated.

BEFORE ACCEPTING The Dorchester Company's offer outright, Mayor LaFortune recommended that the City Commission ask for a second round of sealed bids.[9] The offer presented itself as a unique opportunity to Joe Coleman and Bruce Ervin of Coleman, Ervin & Associates, two downtown architects who had watched in disbelief as the wave of Urban Renewal demolitions swept through their city. Coleman and Ervin had already made a name for themselves as contemporary architects and engineers when they'd decided to push back against the popular belief that demolition was the only economically and culturally viable path to progressive modern

Façade of the **Municipal Building** in late 1972, before renovation. In the background, the 40-story First National Bank of Tulsa tower (known today as First Place Tower) can be seen under construction. OLD CITY HALL BUILDING ARCHIVE

Joe Coleman. COURTESY OF CATHY GILMORE

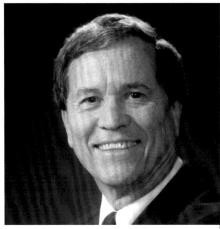

Bruce Ervin. COURTESY OF STEVE ERVIN

Joe Coleman & Bruce Ervin.

Bruce Ervin's daughter, Debi Friggel, said her father and his business partner for 43 years, Joe Coleman, "were like a married couple. Very different personalities—Joe was the people person, my dad more the back-office guy. And they could get frustrated with each other. But they always worked it out."

At the time Coleman, Ervin & Associates acquired the Municipal Building, these two men of contradictions were best known for their modernist architecture. Yet true to their contradictory nature, it is fair to say there would be fewer historical buildings in Tulsa had it not been for their work as preservationists. Today, that balanced view of architecture doesn't seem so unusual. But not so at the time. That was the era when Tulsa's history was being demolished faster than new construction could replace it. Coleman and Ervin bucked the trend and found solutions to adapt buildings with heritage to modern uses. Among their other projects were the Adams Hotel, the Public Service Building, and the Old Central High School.

development. In the Municipal Building, they found an opportunity to lead by example.

Coleman, who had recently served as street commissioner, still had good connections inside city government. With the recommendation of Tulsa's then-street commissioner, Sid Patterson, Coleman submitted a bid for the Municipal Building in August 1972.[10] The Dorchester Company surprised the Commission by electing *not* to submit a bid, thus handing Coleman an easy win.[11] He and the Commission closed the deal in September 1972 for only $150,000. It was a great price made better, ironically, because the official

COLEMAN *&* ERVIN DECIDED *to* PUSH BACK AGAINST *the* BELIEF *that* DEMOLITION *was the* ONLY VIABLE PATH *to* PROGRESSIVE DEVELOPMENT.

In the MUNICIPAL BUILDING, THEY FOUND *an* OPPORTUNITY *to* LEAD *by* EXAMPLE.

Coleman *(left)* and Ervin in 1978 discussing plans to renovate the Adams Hotel. TULSA WORLD

OLD CITY HALL

INDEX

ARCHITECTURAL

COVER SHEET — INDEX
A-1 SITE PLAN
A-2 PLAZA DETAILS
A-3 FIRST FLOOR PLAN
A-4 SECOND FLOOR PLAN
A-5 THIRD FLOOR PLAN
A-6 FOURTH FLOOR PLAN
A-7 INTERIOR ELEVATIONS
A-8 INTERIOR ELEVATIONS
A-9 MILLWORK DETAILS
A-10 MILLWORK DETAILS

MECHANICAL

M-1 BASEMENT MECH PLAN
M-2 FIRST FLOOR MECH PLAN
M-3 SECOND FLOOR MECH PLAN
M-4 THIRD FLOOR MECH PLAN
M-5 FOURTH FLOOR MECH PLAN
M-6 ROOF MECH PLAN AND DETAILS
M-7 MECHANICAL DETAILS

ELECTRICAL

E-1 BASEMENT ELECTRICAL PLAN
E-2 FIRST FLOOR ELECTRICAL PLAN
E-3 SECOND FLOOR ELECTRICAL PLAN
E-4 THIRD FLOOR ELECTRICAL PLAN
E-5 FOURTH FLOOR ELECTRICAL PLAN
E-6 LIGHTING FIXTURE SCHEDULE AND RISER DIAGRAM

COLEMAN · ERVIN · HARRINGTON / ARCHITECTS · ENGINEERS

Planning a Renovation

This collection of original sketches and concept renderings show Coleman and Ervin's work developing the adaptation of the Municipal Building to its current use as a modern office space. The rendering to the far right was done about 10 years later by HTB, the architectural firm charged with the Mid-Continent Tower project *(see page 125)*.

ALL IMAGES: OLD CITY HALL BUILDING ARCHIVE

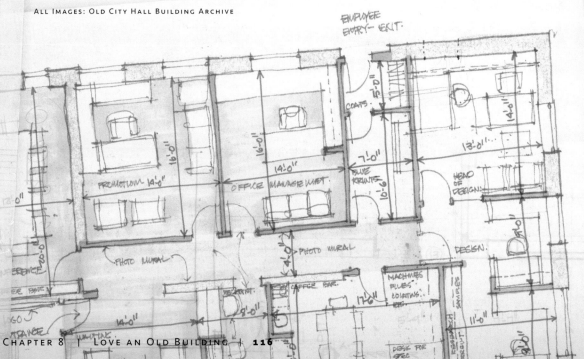

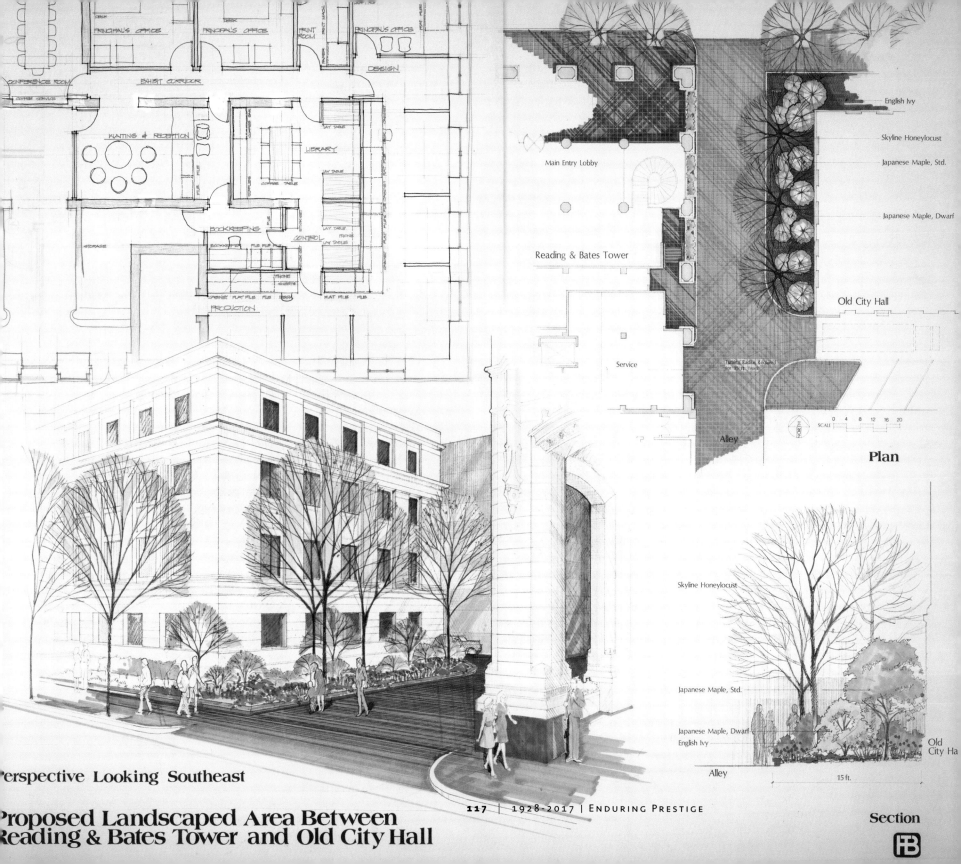

Main Entry Lobby

Reading & Bates Tower

Service

English Ivy

Skyline Honeylocust

Japanese Maple, Std.

Japanese Maple, Dwarf

Old City Hall

Tunnel Radius Required for 35 ft. Truck

Alley

NORTH   SCALE   0   4   8   12   16   20

Plan

Skyline Honeylocust

Japanese Maple, Std.

Japanese Maple, Dwarf
English Ivy

Old City Hall

Alley   15 ft.

Perspective Looking Southeast

Proposed Landscaped Area Between Reading & Bates Tower and Old City Hall

Section

appraiser included a $30,000 demolition allowance, based on the assumption that the building devalued the lot.[12]

Realizing he and Ervin would need a partner to help fund the estimated $650,000 renovation costs, Coleman approached Charles Kothe, John Eagleton, Jerry Nichols, and Skip Wolfe with the law firm of Kothe & Eagleton, Inc. Although initially reluctant, Kothe and Eagleton entertained the proposal, because they were rapidly outgrowing their offices in the mezzanine of the Philtower. Coleman's enthusiasm for the project overcame their skepticism, and the two companies formed a 50/50 partnership for both the purchase of the Municipal Building and its renovation. "It was a great relationship, due to their honesty and vision," Jerry Nichols recalled in a 2017 interview. "They were architects and we were lawyers. Kind of like, do you want a pound of blood or a pound of gold? They were always coming up with something better."[13]

Tulsa watched with great interest and enthusiasm as Coleman and Ervin spent all of 1973 engaged in the monumental task of completely remaking the interior of the Municipal Building. As the work took shape, the media spotlight provided Coleman with the perfect platform to extol the virtues of his preservation philosophies. In a piece he penned for the *Tulsa Tribune*'s Point of View column, Coleman wrote, "The key to the success of preservation efforts lies not in the elimination of demolition and Urban Renewal, but in a merging of the two to shape a future community that will give us the best of the old and the best of the new."[14]

A New Lease on Life.

Old City Hall Building's Open House, March 15, 1974. Dignitaries and public officials enjoyed a new experience involving a historic building in Tulsa. Rather than witness dynamite turn a one-time important piece of property (such as the Hotel Tulsa, or Medical Arts Building) into rubble, they gathered to celebrate a renovation and rejuvenation. While one real-estate professional deemed the property at 4th & Cincinnati worth more without the four-story Municipal Building upon it, Joe Coleman and Bruce Ervin, along with the law firm of Kothe & Eagleton, saw a building that could not only be preserved, but also enhanced. A $650,000 renovation proved their vision was not cloudy.

ALL IMAGES: OLD CITY HALL BUILDING ARCHIVE

FACING PAGE

Left to right: Mayor Robert J. LaFortune, Charles Kothe, Gov. Henry Bellmon, Joe Coleman, and the Rev. Warren Hultgren, First Baptist Church pastor, smile for the camera.

TOP

Among the dignitaries were *(far left)* former Mayor James M. Hewgley, *(third from left)* Mayor LaFortune, *(center)* former Mayor L.C. Clark and former City Auditor Elizabeth Stowell Anderson, *(right of Anderson)* Street Commissioner Sid Patterson, and *(in the background)* the Rev. Warren Hultgren.

ABOVE, LEFT

Among the welcoming crowd that day could be found Street Commissioner Sid Patterson *(left)* with former Mayor James M. Hewgley next to former Mayor L.C. Clark. On the stairs in the light sport coat was television reporter Doug McAllister.

ABOVE, RIGHT

The halls were crowded with people celebrating a building's rebirth.

RIGHT

The Tulsa Flag displayed by *(from left)* Charles Kothe, Mayor Robert J. LaFortune, and Joe Coleman.

Modern Office Space.

The Municipal Building, officially renamed the "Old City Hall Building" as it appeared in 1974, after renovation. The offices of Coleman, Ervin & Associates were located on the first floor *(facing page, top images, and lower far right)*, the offices of Kothe & Eagleton, Inc. were located on the fourth floor. The second and third floors held Williams Brothers subsidiaries of Resources Sciences Corporation.

LEFT AND FACING PAGE: TULSA HISTORICAL SOCIETY

For posterity (and perhaps a little fun), Coleman and Ervin left a few unique, but otherwise unnecessary features from the old City Hall days. On the sides of the lobby staircase can still be found teller windows for paying utility bills, and, on several of the floors, the original vaults serve as closets.

JOHN AMATUCCI

"CLASS" OF '19 ...mural by Delbert L. Jackson

Jackson used the faces of real people from his life or Tulsa's history in the mural. *Left to right:* **Lucille** and **Delbert Jackson** in the red Model T; the police officer is **J.D. Pilkington**; the businessman escorting the lady is Tulsa Oilman, **Julius Livingston** with **Barbara Fulps,** an Amaco Production employee; **W.E."Dode" McIntosh**, Indian Chief and WWI veteran; **Beryl Ford**, Tulsa historian *(far right in group of three men)*; the Cub Scout is **Raid Elauf**, the son of Ata Elauf, an architect on the Old City Hall project. JOHN AMATUCCI

Municipal Building Memories—A bit of playful ribbing might have cost Old City Hall its Delbert Jackson mural. After watching Jackson labor on the piece for six long months, Skip Wolfe jokingly asked him if he ever intended to finish it. Failing to see the humor in the comment, Jackson decided that Wolfe's perceived impatience made him unsure whether or not he even wanted to finish it. Mr. Wolfe was later ushered into an office and politely asked to, "leave the artist alone."

"Class of '19."

The prominent location left bare by the removal of the Municipal Building's 1919 mural is, today, adorned by an even more remarkable replacement. As a counterpoint to the original mural that looked *forward* to a hoped-for future, the current mural is a nostalgic look *back* to 1919—the year the building opened to the public *(see page 68)*. Titled "Class of '19," the enormous 26-by-16-foot, panoramic depiction of the corner of 4th & Cincinnati is the work of **Delbert L. Jackson**, one of Tulsa's most underappreciated artistic talents. Jackson, who spent 31 years as a staff illustrator with Amoco, is best remembered for his 56-foot 1965 masterpiece, "The Panorama of Petroleum" which stood as a permanent feature in the Smithsonian before coming home to Tulsa's International Airport.

To bring the Old City Hall commission to life, Jackson studied historical photos, documents, and materials from which he could sample colors. All the characters represented in the mural are based on real people either from Tulsa's history or Jackson's life. The police officer is the 6'5" J.D. Pilkington, known in 1919 as Tulsa "Chief of Traffic" *(see page 31)*. Jackson painted himself and his wife, Lucille, in a 1915 Model T—a model year Jackson said he chose, in part, because, "the 1915 Model T and I were produced the same year." Also depicted is Tulsa's grandfather of history, Beryl Ford.

On March 15, 1974, the Municipal Building, officially rebranded as the "Old City Hall Building," opened to great fanfare and media attention. Former mayors Clark, Maxwell, and Hewgley joined Mayor LaFortune and a long list of other prominent citizens, politicians, and members of the media to celebrate the rebirth of the faithful old building that had been given a second opportunity to continue a life that seemed to be lived against every odd.

Not only was the grand reopening a media success, it also proved Coleman's argument for the value of adaptive reuse. More than three months before the project's completion, the Old City Hall Building was already 100 percent leased.[15] In addition to the space retained by Coleman, Ervin & Associates, and Kothe & Eagleton, Inc., Resources Sciences Corporation signed leases for their subsidiaries, Williams Brothers Process Services, Inc., and the Map Drafting Department of Williams Brothers Engineering Company.

WITH THE OLD CITY HALL BUILDING standing as a testament to the profitability of renovation over demolition, Coleman and Ervin suddenly found themselves in demand for projects

Jerry R. Nichols.

Frank B. Wolfe III.

EVENTUALLY BUYING OUT *the* OTHER PARTNERS *in the* FIRM, NICHOLS *and* WOLFE WOULD HOLD *on to* OLD CITY HALL *for the* NEXT TWENTY-FIVE YEARS.

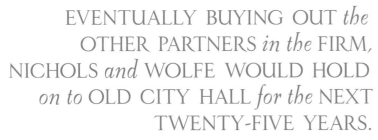

Municipal Building Memories—"One morning, I got down here real early in the morning and I answered the phone and a lady said, 'Who am I speaking to?' and I said, 'It's Buddy Fallis,' and she said, 'You got some people camping on your roof.' Sure enough, some kids coming by bus or hitchhiking got up there and camped out on the roof, and then went to the soup kitchen to eat free." Fallis and others also report the need to occasionally roust an overnight "visitor" sleeping in the flower bed around the building.

all around Tulsa. In February of 1979, Coleman announced their intention to sell Old City Hall to help finance other ongoing projects, including the Adams Hotel at 4th & Boulder. As Coleman explained to *Tulsa World* business writer Linda Martin, "We've completed the creative work and feel the building should be put in the hands of professional, management-type people."[16]

Instead of letting the building go, Coleman and Ervin's partners—since realigned as Nichols, Wolfe, Stamper, Nally & Fallis—decided to purchase the full interest in the partnership, thus assuming total ownership of Old City Hall. Coleman and Ervin went on to numerous adaptive reuse projects that saved many of Tulsa's oil boom-era landmarks, like the entire 600 block of South Main, a project that included the 1929 Public Service Building by architects Arthur Atkinson and Joseph Koberling Jr., Coleman and Ervin's crowning achievement was the dramatic conversion of the old Central High School building at 6th & Cincinnati into the headquarters for the Public Service Company of Oklahoma.

Eventually buying out the other partners in the firm, Nichols and Wolfe would hold on to Old City Hall for the next twenty-five years. During that time, they received several tempting offers to sell, none of which they accepted. On two occasions, however, they did come very close.

The first occasion came in the mid-1980s, when a real-estate broker anxiously approached them with an outstanding offer from an unnamed buyer. Although Nichols and Wolfe were reluctant, the broker worked on them for weeks, never once giving up the name of his client. They strongly considered what had evolved into an exceptionally generous offer, but they ultimately decided they were still too attached to the old building. Once it was clear there would be no deal, the broker confessed, "Roger Hardesty will be very disappointed."[17]

The second occasion came in 2003, when, once again, an enthusiastic real-estate broker approached them ready to make a deal. All the broker was willing to say about this prospective buyer was that they were a big California-based organization interested in establishing a Tulsa headquarters from which to expand operations across the region. They were a very religious group, the broker explained, and felt the "majesty of the building" offered an excellent showcase for their operations.[18]

Jerry Nichols knew very little about the organization vying for his building, and he found no comfort in the few interactions he had with them. As Nichols explained, "They had four or five different people visit the building for days at a time. I got enough out of them to determine that they intended to cut up at least half of those nice, spacious offices to build little closet-like rooms for some kind of one-on-one sessions."[19] Although he didn't like the deal, the broker's offer was solid, and it was coming at a time when both he and Wolfe knew they were ready to sell.

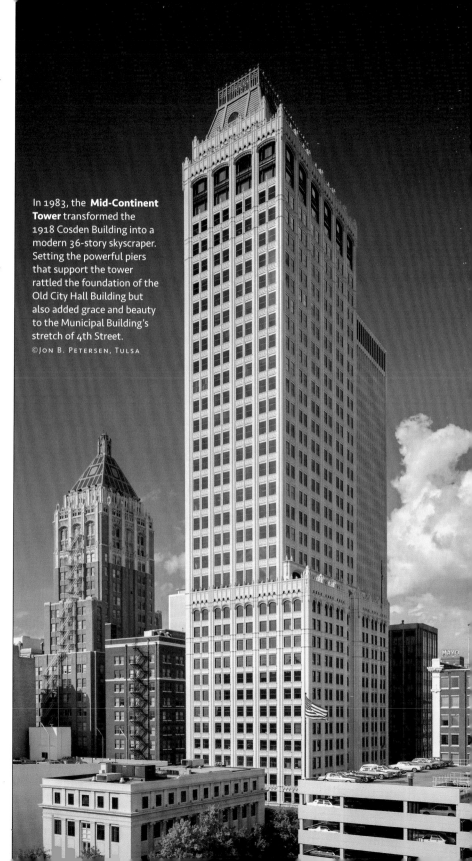

In 1983, the **Mid-Continent Tower** transformed the 1918 Cosden Building into a modern 36-story skyscraper. Setting the powerful piers that support the tower rattled the foundation of the Old City Hall Building but also added grace and beauty to the Municipal Building's stretch of 4th Street.
©Jon B. Petersen, Tulsa

Still preferring to turn the building over to a buyer of their choosing— someone local who would appreciate its significance to Tulsa—they instead offered to sell Old City Hall to an accomplished Tulsa attorney named Frederic Dorwart, who was, at the time, the building's largest tenant and someone they knew had already formed quite an attachment to the place.

Dorwart's relationship with Old City Hall began in 1994, when he and three other attorneys, Tom Murphy, Mike Medina, and Rick Cipolla, started their own practice. At the personal recommendation of one of their clients, George Kaiser, Dorwart and his partners moved into a first-floor suite that Steve Largent's campaign had recently vacated following his successful 1994 run for Oklahoma's 1st Congressional District. With an exceptional list of up-and-coming clients, Dorwart's firm prospered and eventually grew from one suite to more than half the building.

To Nichols and Wolfe, Dorwart was the most logical buyer, and their best bet at finding a good caretaker for the building's heritage. "We told Fred that he's the guy who ought to be buying the building," Nichols recalled. "I told him I had a buyer, but that I'd give him a shot at it if he wanted it, but otherwise I'd take him out of the race. He said no, it is just not a good time."[20]

Both Nichols and Wolfe were so sure Dorwart was the right fit, it took some effort to convince them otherwise. But, once they accepted "no" as his

TO NICHOLS *and* WOLFE, DORWART *was the* MOST LOGICAL BUYER, *and* THEIR BEST BET *at* FINDING *a* GOOD CARETAKER *for the* BUILDING'S HERITAGE.

answer, they reluctantly drew up the sales contract for the mysterious West Coast buyer who turned out to be none other than the Church of Scientology.

At the time, Scientologists were engaged in a push to dramatically expand their number of churches, which they call "Ideal Orgs." Old City Hall would have been of interest to them because the organization had long-favored renovated hotels and office buildings. Before their move on Old City Hall, they had already acquired fifty-four such properties across the world.[21]

Although no direct records regarding their specific plans are accessible, it appears the intention was to convert the Old City Hall Building in to an Ideal Org from which they could establish Tulsa as a central United States hub for the propagation of Scientology.

THE DAY AFTER drawing up the contract, Nichols and Wolfe sat down for lunch with two friends and professional associates, Monty Butts, and his partner, Keith Goddard. During their casual conversation, Nichols shared their intention to sell Old City Hall. As Nichols recalled, Goddard jumped up out of his chair and said, "You're going to sell the building?"

"The deal is on my desk," explained Nichols. "We just have to sign the contract and it's sold."

"Don't sign the contract," Goddard implored. "We've got to buy that building!"

At nine the next morning, Goddard called Nichols to say, "We'll pay more than you're going to sell it for."

"And so, they bought it," said Nichols as he relayed the story years later. "I could not believe it, but they were wired on that deal."

Goddard and Butts only held on to the building until the timing was right for Dorwart to make the logical move of acquiring the property. That time came only two years later, when, in 2006, he purchased Old City Hall.

What drew Scientologists to Tulsa?

At the time the Church of Scientology attempted to purchase the Municipal Building in 2003, it was in the midst of an multi-billion dollar facility expansion program that included the acquisition and renovation of dozens of historical buildings around the world. Launched by controversial Scientology ecclesiastical leader David Miscavige, the intention of the program was to use the prestige of local historic properties "with presence" to bolster the legitimacy of a religion that had scarcely more than a 50-year history. According to Church of Scientology International spokesman, Tommy Davis, "These [buildings] have already been in their cities for many years and need to be large enough to accommodate all their activities, including a chapel, rooms for the study of our theology, and introductory courses for new people and individual spiritual counseling rooms."

Since that time, Frederic Dorwart, Lawyers PLLC, has grown into a firm of more than forty attorneys, which occupies the entire building.

As anticipated by Nichols and Wolfe, Frederic Dorwart has been the ideal caretaker of the old Municipal Building—not merely because he and his firm have been diligent in the never-ending task of maintaining and, in the words of the unknown street philosopher, *loving an old building*, but also because he and the members of his firm share a corporate understanding of the Municipal Building's historical significance and the symbolism it still holds in the community. More than mere lofty words and good intentions, that state of mind has translated into the firm's long-standing commitment to doing work that services the community and contributes to the ongoing development of Tulsa.

Frederic Dorwart, Lawyers PLLC, 2017

More than forty attorneys along with their support staff now call the Old City Hall Building their professional home. Listed in the Bar Register of Preeminent Lawyers, the firm specializes in securities and oil and gas transactions, financial law, and complex business litigation. In keeping with the spirit of the building they occupy, they continue a tradition of donating substantial pro bono services to promote the social, civic, and business development of the Tulsa community. John Amatucci

In the same spirit that J.M. Hall and Reverend Mowbray fought to establish governance as a foundation for civic decency, and in which Mayor Simmons worked to build a physical monument to those ideals, Joe Coleman and Bruce Ervin assumed responsibility for the legacy of the Municipal Building by making it an epicenter for both preservation *and* development. Today, at one hundred years of age, the Municipal Building is still living out its intended purpose as an epicenter for the rule of law, social justice, civic pride, and future community development.

Old City Hall Building, 2017.

ONE HUNDRED YEARS AFTER *the*
LAYING *of its* CORNERSTONE *and* FORTY-FIVE YEARS
SINCE ESCAPING *the* WRECKING BALL,
the NOBLE BUILDING STANDS *as* PROUD *as* EVER
and REMAINS *as* USEFUL *as* EVER—LIVING OUT
ITS INTENDED PURPOSE *as an* EPICENTER *for*
the RULE *of* LAW, SOCIAL JUSTICE, CIVIC PRIDE,
and FUTURE COMMUNITY DEVELOPMENT.

> J·H·SIMMONS — MAYOR
> COMMISSIONERS
> A·W·BRINK
> A·D·WALKER
> C·S·YOUNKMAN
> A·L·FUNK
> ERECTED · A · D · 1917

WHAT MAKES *a* CITY HALL?

T HE READER HAS NO DOUBT recognized the frequent use of the word "irony" in telling the story of Tulsa's seat of power. Truly, there are not many stories from Tulsa's unique history that do not, in some way, invite the use of that word. Thus, it seems appropriate to end this story with yet another twist of irony concerning Tulsa's City Hall. ¶ During the long struggle to build the Municipal Building, Tulsa's city offices remained trapped in leased commercial office space—most notably the dreadful Reeder Building. Even if conditions in the Reeder had not been as bad as they were, Tulsa's boosters still

One Technology Center

West side of Cincinnati between 1st & 2nd Street.
With the acquisition of "the most technologically
advanced building in Oklahoma," Tulsa walked
away from City Hall Tower after a mere
38 years. In doing so, the city
also walked away from the
hard-fought fulfillment of
the multi-generational dream
of a unified Civic Center.
DOUGLAS MILLER

deemed commercial space fully inappropriate for the unique function of a public building—especially one tasked with representing the dignity of a growing and prosperous "Magic City." Yet, once Tulsa had acquired its stately public edifice at 4th & Cincinnati, the growth and success of the Roaring Twenties overshadowed the dignity of a single Municipal Building, leaving those same boosters hungering instead for yet a grander vision of a monumental civic center that would consolidate the prowess and prestige of city, county, state, and federal government. Taking the words of Harland

A *Tulsa Tribune* article from July 13, 1988 outlines what was, at the time, merely the latest round of "extensive repairs" required in the Civic Center's first twenty years alone. TULSA TRIBUNE

Bartholomew fully to heart: "A civic center that is well-located, adequate in size, and outstanding in design is an asset which increases in value as the years pass. A cheap compromise will soon become a matter of deep regret," Tulsa's movers and shakers—private sector, government, and citizens alike—spent forty-five of the Municipal Building's fifty years of service pursuing the brass ring of a civic center grand enough to garner global attention. Yet once grasped, the brass ring quickly tarnished.

Despite costing enough to avoid Bartholomew's warning of "a cheap compromise," *(see page 98)* many aspects of Tulsa's Civic Center made it "a matter of deep regret." More than thirty years of coping with engineering oversights, dysfunctional fountains, drainage problems, material failures, asbestos, and the public's disinterest in plazas left the city with $24 million in deferred maintenance and a second dream—*getting out* of the Civic Center.

The best opportunity to leave came during the administration of Tulsa's thirty-eighth mayor, Kathy Taylor. Despite having embraced nearly 100 years of anthropological and architectural philosophies on the unique physical and cultural role of purpose-built public buildings and open public spaces, the grand solution to the Civic Center problem, it seems, was a return to commercial office space surrounded by high urban density.

In 2007, as Frederic Dorwart was settling in as the new owner of the Municipal Building, Mayor Taylor was proposing a $67.1-million acquisition she called a, "once-in-a-lifetime, transformational opportunity" to move City Hall to One Technology Center, the 15-story former headquarters of Tulsa's Williams Communications. If approved, it would be the first time Tulsa bestowed the honorable title of "City Hall" on commercial office space since it escaped the Reeder Building at the beginning of 1919.

$300,000 immediate Center need

By ANNA AMERICA
Tribune Writer

It will take $300,000 in short-term repairs to make the Tulsa Civic Center parking and plaza complex safe and $11 million in the long run to refurbish it, a citizens committee was told Tuesday.

Dozens of sections of the three-level parking garage and plaza have been closed off since June 7 because structural deterioration made them unsafe.

Contractors are repairing a sidewalk section in front of the Maxwell Convention Center where falling cement left a 1½-foot hole through to the basement garage below.

A consulting group has been studying the condition and uses of the Civic Center and this fall is expected to make a final report on what steps should be taken to prevent further deterioration.

Preliminary repair estimates were presented Tuesday to the Civic Center Citizens Advisory Committee, made up of about 20 private, business and government representatives. Streets Commissioner J.D. Metcalfe said cost es-

Tribune photo by Buddy Mangine
'orkers patch sidewalk outside Convention Center.

See CENTER, page 4A

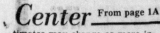

Center From page 1A

timates may change as more information is gathered.

The Civic Center was completed in 1969. It has had extensive repairs several times; officials say the same kind of deterioration is occurring in this type of buildings all over the country because of the heavy traffic load and because much of the surface area is exposed to the elements.

Metcalfe said he will begin this

concrete slabs in the floors of the plaza and parking levels with modern, weatherproofed materials and watertight membranes.

That plan would cost about $11 million, $9.5 million for the city's portion of the complex and $1.5 million for the county's portion, said Daryl Radcliffe, lead structural engineer for the consulting project.

The figure does not include the cost of design changes to make the center more functional. The consultants also are studying that area.

Metcalfe said the $11 million probably would have to come through a bond issue or an extension of the temporary third-penny sales tax that is used for capital improvements.

Calling that solution the ideal

The beleaguered Reeder Building only survived ten years after City Hall moved out. It was mercifully put out of its misery in 1929 when it was replaced with the beautiful 10-story Bliss Hotel. The elegant terracotta crown of the Bliss graced the city's skyline until falling victim of Urban Renewal in 1969. Today, the very same land along 2nd Street once occupied by the Reeder Building and the Bliss is now covered by the southeast corner of the BOK Tower and (here's the promised irony) One Technology Center—the commercial office space that has served as Tulsa's official City Hall since the spring of 2008.

Ghost of the Reeder Building.

More than just the city's first return to commercial office space since it escaped the Reeder Building in 1919, City Hall's 2008 move to One Technology Center also returned Tulsa's seat of power to the 2nd Street location where the Reeder Building once stood. Fortunately, location is the only similarity shared by the two buildings.

TULSA'S SEAT *of* POWER EVOLVED *from the* COUNCIL OAK TREE, *to the* MUNICIPAL BUILDING, CITY HALL TOWER, *and then* ONE TECHNOLOGY CENTER. *For as* COMPLETELY DIFFERENT *as* EACH *of* THESE FOUR CENTERS *of* MUNICIPAL GOVERNMENT ARE, *they all* SUCCEEDED *in* REPRESENTING *the* TULSA *of* THEIR ERA.

Considered to be the most technologically advanced building in the state, it was, indeed, a move that would redefine Tulsa's long-standing view of what makes a city hall. As explained in *Lives of Vision, Mission & Loyalty: The Lobeck Taylor Story*, "Centralization of services had been the primary goal when the [Civic Center] complex was built in 1964. But as Tulsa grew, those services began to be extended, and the previous rationale for the centralization of government activities wore thin." Although the debt the city incurred made the move controversial, Taylor's successor, Tulsa's thirty-ninth mayor, Dewey F. Bartlett Jr., proved the value of the building when he offloaded a considerable portion of One Technology Center's debt by selling floors that were unused by the city to Magellan Midstream Partners, LP, the tenant that had already been occupying them. In addition to the direct financial benefit to the City of Tulsa, the move also anchored nearly one thousand high-income jobs to downtown Tulsa.

"Technology has forever changed the way citizens interact with their government," Bartlett explained in 2017. "And it's also changed the way various government entities interact with each other. Not only is there no longer a practical need for city, county, state, and federal government to be next door to work synergistically, but the unique technological aspects of One Technology Center have made Tulsa's City Hall more accessible than it's ever been."

Regarding the role City Hall has in reflecting the prestige and character of its community, Bartlett noted that visitors to Tulsa are often taken aback by the building. "They'll say things like, 'I can't believe this is your City Hall!' I could walk someone all the way around the outside edge of the fifteenth floor and give them an entire panoramic tour of Tulsa—from the river to the airport—without ever leaving the building. Visitors are always very impressed. There really isn't another City Hall quite like it."

IT IS REMARKABLE to ponder how Tulsa's seat of power evolved from the Council Oak Tree, to the Municipal Building, City Hall Tower, and then One Technology Center. For as completely different as each of these four longest-serving centers of municipal government are from each other, they all succeeded in one commonality: representing the Tulsa of their era. One other remarkable thing cannot be taken for granted: all four of these hallmarks of Tulsa's official relationship between her people and her government are still standing, still in use, and still serving the public, each in their own way.

This last point underscores the importance of the Municipal Building's survival. Historical preservation was the expressed intention of Coleman

and Ervin when they saved the Municipal Building from the wrecking ball. Likewise, it was interested citizens, not mayors or politicians, who intervened to preserve both City Hall Tower and the Council Oak Tree.

Operating under the name Brickhugger, LLC., Tulsa's Snyder Family renovated City Hall Tower in 2013, reopening it as a modern Aloft Hotel. And, in 1978, H.D. "Nat" Henshaw organized his neighbors to save the Council Oak Tree from a developer's bulldozer. While all three sites are now protected by listings on the National Register of Historic Places, the credit for their survival is due to the investment and action of regular Tulsans. What inspired them? Perhaps it was the passion that Tulsa now has for the preservation of its historical places. And the genesis for that passion might well be credited to the influential role the preservation of the Municipal Building had on changing Tulsa's view of its own history. ■

ABOVE LEFT

Council Oak Park, 2014. In the 1960s, the Council Oak Tree, Tulsa's most valuable historic site, was on the verge of being bulldozed for the development of a mere parking lot. The requested zoning change resulted in a legal contest that saved the tree by eventually pushing the land into foreclosure. In 1978, local resident H.D. "Nat" Henshaw organized his neighbors and purchased the lot at the sheriff's sale for the purpose of forever preserving the site. Today, the park is owned by the City of Tulsa and the Council Oak Tree is listed in the National Register of Historic Places. The land development that once threatened the site ultimately became the OakClaire Townhomes, another Coleman, Ervin & Associates project. DOUGLAS MILLER

ABOVE RIGHT

Downtown Tulsa's Aloft Hotel was the second major redevelopment project spearheaded by Tulsa's Snyder family's Brickhugger, LLC. The first was the tremendously successful redevelopment of the beautiful 1925 Mayo Hotel at 115 West 5th Street. TDL NOW, LLC

A 1997 painting of the Old City Hall Building by Tulsa artist **Gail Booth**. The painting was commissioned by Frederic Dorwart's wife, Nanu, as a gift for his 60th birthday.

NOTES

CHAPTER ONE

1) **As related here, the story of the deaths of Thomas Jefferson Archer and Andrew Perryman was compiled from the following sources:**

J.M. Hall, *The Beginning of Tulsa* (Tulsa, c.1933), 17–18.

Nina Lane Dunn, *Tulsa's Magic Roots* (Tulsa: Oklahoma Publishing Company, 1979), 357–58.

Angie Debo, *Tulsa: From Creek Town to Oil Capital* (Norman: University of Oklahoma Press, 1943), 73–74.

Susan Everly-Douze, *Tulsa Times: A Pictorial History: The Early Years* (Tulsa: World Publishing Company, 1986), 101.

Nancy Schallner, "Tulsa Pioneer: T.J. Archer," Tulsa Gal, November 18, 2009 (accessed May 8, 2017), www.tulsagal.net.

Nancy Schallner, "T.J. Archer, Part 2," Tulsa Gal, November 27, 2009 (accessed May 8, 2017), www.tulsagal.net.

"A Can of Powder Explodes at Tulsa, Killing the Chief's Son," *The Indian Journal* (Eufaula, Oklahoma), November 2, 1894.

"Killed by a Powder Explosion," *Muskogee Phoenix*, November 3, 1894.

"Exploding Powder," *Weekly Chieftain* (Vinita, Oklahoma), November 8, 1894.

2) Edward Everett and Morris L. Dale Wardell, *The History of Oklahoma* (Englewood Cliffs: Prentice-Hall, 1948), 286–287.

3) Glenn Shirley, *Frontier Marshal: The Story of a Real Gunfighter* (Philadelphia: Chilton Co., Book Division, 1962), 190.

4) Wishard Lemons, *The First Hundred* (Tulsa: First United Methodist Church, 1987), p.37.

5) Shirley, 91–101, 138.

6) "Strong Drink the Cause," *Girard Press*, January 17, 1895.

7) Ibid.

8) Shirley, 182.

9) Ibid., 186–87.

10) Lemons, 35.

CHAPTER TWO

1) Acts of the Fifty-Third Congress–Third Session, 1895. Chapter 188.

2) Angie Debo, *Tulsa: From Creek Town to Oil Capital* (Norman: University of Oklahoma Press, 1943), 78.

3) *The Baxter Springs News*, December 18, 1897.

4) Col. Clarence B. Douglas, *History of Tulsa, Oklahoma* (Chicago-Tulsa: The S.J. Clarke Publishing Company Co., 1921), 583.

5) *The Indian Republican*.

6) Ronald L. Trekell, *History of the Tulsa Police Department*, 1882-1990 (Tulsa: The Dept., 1989), 21.

7) "Col. E. Calkins," *The Tulsa New Era*, vol. 3, March 10, 1895.

8) J.M. Hall, *The Beginning of Tulsa* (Tulsa, c.1933), 92.

9) Nina Lane Dunn, *Tulsa's Magic Roots* (Tulsa: The Oklahoma Publishing Company, 1979), 276.

10) Ibid.

11) Hall, 69.

12) Ibid.

13) "Pictorially Presenting Greater Tulsa (Tulsa: The Chamber of Commerce, 1923), 2.

CHAPTER THREE

1) Doug Hicks, *Nearly Forgotten* (Tulsa: Schnake Turnbo Frank, Inc., 2005), 2.

2) Douglas Miller, *4th & Boston: Heart of the Magic Empire* (Tulsa: Müllerhaus Legacy, 2016), 88.

3) Nina Lane Dunn, *Tulsa's Magic Roots* (Tulsa: The Oklahoma Publishing Company, 1979), 168.

4) Dunn, 261.

5) **The question of passing bonds was hit and miss until Oklahoma's State Constitution clarified the law. Tulsa Public Schools passed its first bond in 1905, but, in 1906, the passage of a $100,000 bond for the purchase of Tulsa's first waterworks was thrown out after challenged in court.** Dunn, 164, 280.

6) Dunn, 279.

7) Dunn, 262.

8) Ronald L. Trekell, *History of the Tulsa Police Department 1882-1990* (Tulsa: The Dept., 1989), 32.

9) Courtney Ann and Glen Vaughn-Roberson, *City in the Osage Hills* (Boulder: Pruett Publishing Company, 1984), 93.

10) Vaughn-Roberson, 94.

11) Trekell, 39.

12) Trekell, 40.

13) "U.S. Marshals Killed by Barber," *Morning Tulsa Daily World*, July 24, 1914.

14) Trekell, 42.

15) Dunn, 276-278.

16) **Because city officials ran nonpartisan races before statehood, Simmons is credited with being Tulsa's first Republican mayor instead of Colonel Calkins.**

17) "Will Expose City Officials' Graft," *Morning Tulsa Daily World*, March 29, 1916.

18) Bill Waller, *History of the Metro Chamber*, 19.

᠎
19) Ibid.

20) Ibid.

21) "Simmons Elected by the Biggest Majority Ever Received by Candidate," *Morning Tulsa Daily World*, April 5, 1916.

CHAPTER FOUR

1) Ronald L. Trekell, *History of the Tulsa Police Department 1882-1990* (Tulsa: The Dept., 1989), 26.

2) "City Hall Foundation Completed," *Tulsa Daily World*, September 14, 1905.

3) Trekell, 26.

4) Ibid.

5) "Extension to City Building to Be Made," *Morning Tulsa Daily World*, June 21, 1906.

6) Nina Lane Dunn, *Tulsa's Magic Roots* (Tulsa: The Oklahoma Publishing Company Co, 1979), 311.

7) "City Hall Located in Reeder Building," *Morning Tulsa Daily World*, June 2, 1912.

8) Ibid.

9) Trekell, 63.

10) "Opponents of Bonds Hope to Win by Stay-at-Home Vote," *Morning Tulsa Daily World*, June 18, 1915.

11) Ibid.

12) "City Hall Plans Are Considered," *Morning Tulsa Daily World*, March 10, 1915.

13) Ibid.

14) Ibid.

15) "Fail to Agree on New City Building," *Morning Tulsa Daily World*, April 15, 1915.

16) "Current Comment," *Morning Tulsa Daily World*, April 17, 1915.

17) "City Hall Badly Needed in Tulsa," *Morning Tulsa Daily World*, May 12, 1915.

18) "Three Big Bond Issues Up to a Vote of People," *Morning Tulsa Daily World*, June 1, 1915.

19) Ibid.

20) Ibid.

21) "Tulsa Retains Reputation of Doing Things," *Morning Tulsa Daily World*, June 19, 1915.

22) "Commissioners Are Almost Flooded Out," *Morning Tulsa Daily World*, June 23, 1915.

CHAPTER FIVE

1) "Tulsa Is Very Bad Old Town," *Wichita Daily Eagle*, November 5, 1915.

2) Ibid.

3) "Too Friendly with Gamblers," *Los Angeles Times*, December 31, 1915.

4) "Two Officials Removed," *Wilmington Morning Star*, December 19, 1915.

5) "15 Indictments in Gambling Trust Inquiry in Tulsa," *St. Louis Post-Dispatch*, December 31, 1915.

6) Ibid.

7) Ibid.

8) "Chief Burns Fired Again," *Democrat-American* (Sallisaw, OK), December 31, 1915.

9) Ronald L. Trekell, *History of the Tulsa Police Department, 1882--1990* (Tulsa: The Dept., 1989), 42.

10) "Near Tragedy at Tulsa City Hall," *Morning Tulsa Daily World*, January 23, 1915.

11) "Now the Sheriff, He's Fired," *Indian Journal* (Eufaula, OK), January 15, 1916.

12) Ibid.

13) "Start City Hall Within 45 Days," *Morning Tulsa Daily World*, July 5, 1916.

14) Ibid.

15) "Continue Hearing in City Jail Case," *Morning Tulsa Daily World*, July 2, 1916.

16) "Tulsa Assured of Municipal Hall," *Morning Tulsa Daily World*, July 20, 1916.

17) "City Jail Now Moves to the Courthouse," *Morning Tulsa Daily World*, July 5, 1916.

18) "Board Favors Elk's Property for City Hall," *Morning Tulsa Daily World*, November 25, 1916.

19) "Church Property for a City Hall?" *Morning Tulsa Daily World*, November 19, 1916.

20) "Select a New Site for High School," *Morning Tulsa Daily World*, July 7, 1915.

21) "City Bids for Plot on School Property," *Morning Tulsa Daily World*, November 2, 1916.

22) "City Gets Deed to Site," *Morning Tulsa Daily World*, December 7, 1916.

23) "City Dads Hope to Make Record," *Morning Tulsa Daily World*, December 10, 1916.

CHAPTER SIX

1) "Start City Hall Within 45 Days," *Morning Tulsa Daily World*, October 6, 1916.

2) "City Hall Plans Are Completed," *Morning Tulsa Daily World*, March 2, 1917.

3) Ibid.

4) Colonel Clarence B. Douglas, *The History of Tulsa, Oklahoma* (Chicago-Tulsa: The S.J. Clarke Publishing Company, 1921), 546.

5) "City Hall Contract Is Held Off Until Friday," *Morning Tulsa Daily World*, May 30, 1917.

6) "No Skyscraper for a While, Avers Simmons," *Morning Tulsa Daily World*, December 9, 1916.

7) **In 1928, another three stories were added to the Hotel Tulsa. The building was demolished in 1970 to make room for Tulsa's Performing Arts Center.**

8) "Beers Company Gets City Hall Contract," *Morning Tulsa Daily World*, June 7, 1917.

9) "Must Complete City Hall by February 1," *Morning Tulsa Daily World*, June 13, 1917.

10) "City Hall Work Delayed Because of School Board," *Morning Tulsa Daily World*, June 30, 1917.

11) "How Tulsa's New Municipal Building is Going to Look," *Morning Tulsa Daily World*, July 1, 1917.

12) "Tulsa Capitulates to Wets; Open-Town Victory at Polls," *Morning Tulsa Daily World*, April 3, 1918.

13) "M'Nulty Is Made Mayor of Tulsa,"
Morning Tulsa Daily World, May 4, 1918.

14) "Building Inspector Will Not Quit Job,"
Morning Tulsa Daily World, June 12, 1918.

15) "Three Months Complete New Municipal Building,"
Morning Tulsa Daily World, June 28, 1918.

16) "City Hall Contract in Tangle Over Extras,"
Morning Tulsa Daily World, August 17, 1918.

17) "New City Hall Will Be Occupied in a Few Days,"
Morning Tulsa Daily World, January 28, 1919.

18) "Marble Fitters at Work Finishing New City Hall,"
Morning Tulsa Daily World, March 20, 1919.

19) "Beautiful Mural Painting Which Represents
'Tulsa, Her Past and Future,' Is Finished by Artist,"
Morning Tulsa Daily World, May 10, 1919.

20) Walter F. White, "The Eruption of Tulsa,"
The Nation, June 29, 1921.

21) Nina Lane Dunn, *Tulsa's Magic Roots* (Tulsa:
The Oklahoma Publishing Company, 1979), 320.

22) Dunn, 320-321.

23) Hannibal B. Johnson, *Black Wall Street*
(Fort Worth: Eakin Press, 1998), 96, 106.

24) "A New Deal," *The Tulsa Spirit*,
(Vol. 7, No. 22, July 1922), 11.

CHAPTER SEVEN

1) Charles L. Hardt, *Draft Environmental Impact
Statement, Proposed East 71st Street South from South
Lewis Avenue to South Memorial Drive* (City of Tulsa,
Oklahoma, 1989), 2.

2) *Bartholomew Report*, 1930.

3) Larry O'Dell, "Patton, Daniel Webster,"
The Encyclopedia of Oklahoma History and Culture,
(accessed July 8, 2017), www.okhistory.org.

4) "Current Comment," *Morning Tulsa Daily World*,
April 17, 1915.

5) Frosty Troy, "Robust Tulsa Bursting 1918 City Hall's
Seams," *Tulsa Tribune*, 1958 (date unavailable).

6) S.M. "Buddy" Fallis (former Tulsa district attorney),
interview by John Hamill, 2017.

7) *Bartholomew Report*, 1930.

8) Tom Birmingham, "Civic Center; a 35-Year-Old
Dream," *Tulsa Tribune*, July 25, 1965.

9) "Civic Center Plan Offered,"
Tulsa Tribune, August 2, 1954.

10) "Formal Plea for New City Hall Site Set,"
Tulsa World, late 1954 (exact date unavailable).

11) Ibid.

12) Ibid.

13) Ibid.

14) Troy.

CHAPTER EIGHT

1) Cathy Ambler, "Tulsa Civic Center Historic District."
(United States Department of the Interior; National
Park Service; National Register of Historic Places
Registration Form, 2011), 13.

2) Siegfried Giedion, *Architektur und Gemeinschaft.
Tagebuch einer Entwicklung*, (Rowohlt, verlag), 1956.

3) "Old City Hall Appears Doomed; Option to Purchase
Disclosed," *Tulsa Tribune*, July 7, 1972.

4) Douglas Miller, *4th & Boston: Heart of the Magic
Empire* (Tulsa: Müllerhaus Legacy, 2016), 241.

5) Ibid.

6) Bob Foresman, "Community Chest Eyes Old City Hall,"
Tulsa Tribune, July 7, 1972.

7) "Old City Hall Appears Doomed; Option to Purchase
Disclosed," *Tulsa Tribune*, July 7, 1972.

8) Clayton Vaughn (former KOTV anchorman),
interview by John Hamill, April 10, 2017.

9) "Old City Hall Appears Doomed; Option to Purchase
Disclosed," *Tulsa Tribune*, July 7, 1972.

10) "Ex-Street Official Buys Old City Hall,"
Tulsa World, c. September 1972.

11) "$150,000 Bid Offered for Old City Hall by Ex-
Commissioner," *Tulsa Tribune*, August 1972.

12) "Ex-Street Official Buys Old City Hall,"
Tulsa World, c. September 1972.

13) Frank B. "Skip" Wolfe III and Jerry Nichols,
interview by John Hamill, April 24, 2017.

14) Undated *Tulsa Tribune* column by Joe Coleman found
in "Old City Hall" memorabilia file.

15) "'Old City Hall' Fully Filled on Refurbishing,"
Tulsa World, December 1973.

16) "Old City Hall Building Up for Sale,"
Tulsa World, February 3, 1979.

17) Frank B. "Skip" Wolfe III and Jerry Nichols,
interview by John Hamill, April 24, 2017.

18) Ibid.

19) Ibid.

20) Ibid.

21) Laurie Goodstein, "Scientology Defectors Speak Out,"
New York Times, March 6, 2010 (accessed July 14,
2017), www.web.archive.org.

INDEX

A

Adams Hotel, 115, 124
Alder, Rolla C., 43, 44
Allen, Clarence, 98
Aloft Hotel, 135, 136
Ames, Glen, 98
Anderson, Elizabeth Stowell, 94, 95, 119
Andrew Carnegie City Library, 32, 33
Archer, Annie Mowbray, 9, 10, 12, 14, 20
Archer, Georgia, 14
Archer, James V., 14
Archer, Mabel G., 14
Archer, Thomas Jefferson "Jeff,"
    4–6, 10, 12, 15, 20
Archer & Boulder, 55
Archer & Detroit, 55
Archer Store, 4–6, 10–12, 20, 28, 60
Archer Street, 86
Architectural League of Tulsa, 88, 101, 104
Architecture, 33, 60, 64, 65, 89
Ardmore, Oklahoma, 7
Arkansas River, 4, 18, 19, 21, 24, 33, 75
Atkinson, Arthur, 124
Atkinson, J.M., 75
Atlas Life Building, 64, 67
Automobile parade, 66
Avery, C.S., 75

B

Ball Memorial Church, 94
Barber, William, 30
Bartholomew, Harland, 85, 86,
    88–90, 98, 102, 134
Bartholomew Report, 86, 88–91, 101
Bartlett, Dewey F., Jr., viii, 136
The Baxter Springs News, 14
Beane-Vandever Dry Goods Company, 40
Beers Construction Company, 65, 66, 71
Bellmon, Henry, 119
Big Six, 50
Bird Creek, 91
Birmingham, Tom, 98, 107, 110
Black Wall Street, 76

Blakely, George, viii
Bliss Hotel, 135
Block 137, 55, 56–57, 78
BOK Tower, 135
Bonds
    bridge, 24
    City Hall, 39, 40, 44–45
    civic center, 107
    Convention Hall (Brady Theater), 39
    infrastructure, 90
    legal implications, 26 n.5, 46, 48, 54
    Municipal Building, 44–45, 65–66
    Spavinaw Water Project, 75, 94
Booth, Gail, 136
Boston Avenue, 21, 37, 40, 86, 87
Boston Avenue Methodist-
    Episcopal Church, 64
Boulder Street, 98
Brady, Tate, 15, 19
Brady Theater. *See* Convention
    Hall (Brady Theater)
Brickhugger, LLC, 135, 136
Brogan, John M., 10
Brown, Mrs. J. Benjamin, 75
Bryan, William Jennings, 16
Building boom, 22, 24, 33, 39–41, 54, 55
Buildings and Building Management, 69, 71
Burns, Foster N., 30, 50
Burns Detective Agency, 50
Butler, Courtland L., 70–71
Butts, Monty, 127
Bynum, G.T., viii
Bynum, R.N., viii, 19, 55, 56

C

Calkins, Edward E., viii, 15–18,
    27, 31, 31 n.16
Calkins, Elenore, 17
Campbell, Harry, 15, 16
Central High School, 56, 67, 115, 124
Central National Bank, 40
Chamber of Commerce, 4, 19–21, 31, 33,
    49, 53, 55, 60, 65–66, 71, 78, 82, 101

Chappelle, T.O., 76
Charter of Incorporation, 15, 31
Cherokee Strip Land Run of 1893, 10
Cheyenne Street, 98
Chicago, 25, 50
Chicago Board of Trade, 25
Chicago School of Architecture, 64
Christian Church, 55
Church of Scientology, 127
Cincinnati Avenue, 86, 87, 135
Cipolla, Rick, 126
City Commission, 33, 55, 70,
    108–110, 114, 115
City Hall
    bonds, 44–45
    City Hall (1906-1909), 23, 38, 39, 69
    City Hall Tower (1969-2007),
        43, 88, 103, 104,
        108, 133, 135
    Council Oak Tree (1836-1861),
        xvii, 38, 136, 137
    daily activities, 94
    Egan Building (1909-1910), 37, 39, 40
    Hall & Co. Store (1882-1897), 3, 4, 38
    Lynch Building (1897-1906), 13, 38, 39
    Municipal Building. *See* Municipal
        Building (1919-1969)
    Old City Hall, 99, 112, 113,
        118, 120, 122–136
    One Technology Center
        (2007-), 43, 133–135
    Reeder Building (1912-1919),
        37, 40, 41, 43, 45–47,
        50, 54, 66, 104, 132–135
    Shutts Building (1910-1912), 37, 40
City Hall Annex, 101
City Hall Tower (1969-2007), 43, 88,
    103, 104, 108, 131, 133–136
City jail, 41, 45, 54
City National Bank, 53
Civic Center, 59, 73–74, 78, 83,
    87–88, 91, 100–101, 103–105,
    107–108, 110, 113, 133–135

Civil War, 16
Clark, L.C., viii, 94–96, 101, 104, 119, 123
Cline, H.R., viii
Clinton, Fred S., 40
Clinton Building, 67, 69
Coleman, Ervin & Associates,
    113–115, 120, 123, 136
Coleman, Joe, 113–116, 118,
    119, 123, 124, 128, 133
Commercial Club, 19–21, 24–27,
    31, 33, 38–40, 44
Conneely, Charles W., 28
Convention Hall (Brady Theater),
    32, 33, 39, 60, 88, 89
Cosden Building, 57, 69, 125
Council Oak Tree (1836-1861),
    xvii, 38, 133, 136
Cox, Burl, 15
Crawford, Dick, viii
Creek Indians, 4, 55
Creek Nation, 6–7, 11, 15
Crime. *See* Vice and crime

D

Dalton, Bob, 8
Dalton, Emmet, 8, 24
Dalton, Grat, 8
Dalton Gang, 7, 8, 10, 20
Daniel Building, 65, 67
Davis, Tommy, 127
Democrat, 26
Denver Street, 98, 101
Depression. *See* Great Depression
Doolin Gang, 8, 10
Dorchester, Don, Jr., 110
Dorchester Company, 110, 114, 115
Dorwart, Frederic, 99, 126, 127, 128, 134
Douglas, Clarence B., xvii, 16, 60
Duncan, Frank, 75
Dunn, Nina Lane, 18

E

E.A. Rush & Company, 64
Eagleton, John, 118
Earp, Wyatt, 7
Egan Building (1909-1910), 37, 39, 40
Elauf, Ata, 122
Elauf, Raid, 122
Elections, 18, 28, 31, 42, 44, 52, 67, 70,
   107.
   See also Politics
Elks Club, 55
Elwood Street, 89
Endacott, Asbury, 64
Ervin, Bruce, 113–116, 118,
   123, 124, 128, 133
Eufaula, Oklahoma, 52
Evans, Thaddeus D., viii, 75–78
Exchange National Bank Building, 90

F

Fallis, S.M. "Buddy," 93, 99, 124, 125
Federal building, 33
Federal Housing Acts
   of 1949 and 1954, 110
5th & Boulder, 78
5th & Cincinnati, 78
5th & Main, 67
5th Street, 89
Figgel, Debi, 115
Fire department, 14–15, 38, 39, 43
First Methodist-Episcopal Church, 8
First National Bank of Tulsa, 50, 53, 69, 114
First Place Tower, 114
First Presbyterian Church of Tulsa, 4
First United Methodist Church, 11
1st & Main Street, 3–5, 13, 39
1st Street, 28, 56
The First Hundred (Lemons), 11
Five Nations, 7, 14
Flag of Tulsa, 119
Flynn, Olney F., viii
Ford, Beryl, 122, 123
Forsythe, Jay, 19, 55, 56

400 Boston Building, 67
Fourth Street Parking garage, 67
4th & Boston, 18
4th & Boulder, 55, 124
4th & Cincinnati, 41, 55, 57, 59, 66,
   110, 118, 123, 126, 134
4th & Main, 30, 67, 68
4th Street, 69, 86, 88, 98, 125
Franklin, B.C., 76
Frederic Dorwart, Lawyers PLLC, 128
Freeling, S. Prince, 48, 49, 54
Frisco Depot, 16, 21
Frisco Railroad, 4, 5, 15, 19, 50
Fulps, Barbara, 122

G

Gallais Building, 54, 67
Gallaway, Paul M., 44–45
Giedion, Sigfried, 104, 105
Gilcrease Museum, 106
Gilmore, Leon, 109
Glenn Pool, 18, 21, 22, 24, 25, 36, 40
Goble, Danney, 107
Goddard, Keith, 127
Goff, Bruce, 64, 78
Grand Opera House, 32, 33
Great Depression, 83, 90, 91, 93, 99, 100
Great Fire of 1897, 14, 15, 38
Greenwood District, 26, 27, 33, 75–77, 101
Griggs, Charles, 75

H

Hall, Harry C., 4
Hall, J.M., xvii, 3–6, 11, 15–19, 21,
   27, 28, 38, 55, 56, 75, 128
Hall & Co. Store (1882-1897), 3, 4, 38
Hardesty, Roger, 125
Harland Bartholomew & Associates
   (HBA), 85, 89, 90
Harp, Bill, 95
Haskell, Charles N., 33
Hell's Half-Acre, 10
Henshaw, H.D. "Nat," 135, 136

Hewgley, James M., Jr.,
   viii, 104, 109, 119, 123
Hicks, Doug, 22
History of Tulsa, Oklahoma (Douglas),
   16, 60
Holderness, Clark, 27
Holderness, Lennie, 27
Holland, C.L., 56–57
Holway, W.R., 75
Hotel Tulsa, 65, 65 n.7, 67, 118
Houston Street, 89
HTB, 116
Hubbard, Charles H., viii, 67,
   70, 71, 75, 77, 104
Hughes, T.C., 75
Hultgren, Warren, 119
Hunt, Oliver D., 45, 50, 52, 70
Hunt Building, 68

I

Indian Journal, 52
Indian Republican, 15
Indian Territory, 5, 7, 11, 14, 18, 19, 26
Infrastructure development,
   14, 26, 28, 31, 65, 85, 90–91
Inhofe, James M., viii
Inner Dispersal Loop (IDL), 84
International Petroleum Exposition
   and Congress, 19, 90

J

Jackson, Delbert L., 122, 123
Jackson, Lucille, 122, 123
Jaycees (Junior Chamber of
   Commerce), 107
Jim Crow laws, 26, 75

K

Kaiser, George, 126
Kennedy, Samuel Grant, 15, 16, 18, 19
Kennedy, Wess, 15
Kennedy Building, 18, 54, 67, 69
Koberling, Joseph, Jr., 124

Kothe, Charles, 118, 119
Kothe & Eagleton, Inc., 118, 120, 123

L

LaFortune, Bill, viii
LaFortune, Robert J., viii, 109,
   114, 119, 123
Largent, Steve, 126
Law enforcement
   cleaning up of Tulsa, 10–11, 14, 18
   Lighthorsemen, 7
   Tulsa as safe harbor, 7
Lawlessness in Tulsa, 6, 7, 30
Lawton, Oklahoma, 8
Lee-Huckins Hotel, 48
Legislation
   Indian Territory, 7, 12, 14
   Tulsa city charter, 26–27
Lemons, Wishard, 11
Lewis, Mrs. S.R., 75
Lighthorsemen, 7
Lindsay, Lilah D., 75
Linn, Conn, 48, 49, 52
Liquor issues, 30, 31, 50, 51
Lives of Vision, Mission & Loyalty:
   The Lobeck Taylor Story, 136
Livingston, Julius, 122
Loachapoka Tallasi, xvii, 15
Lorton, Eugene, 75
Lundy, Roy B., viii, 84
Lynch, C.B., 13
Lynch, R.E., 15, 19
Lynch Building (1897-1906), 13, 38, 39
Lyric Theater, 13

M

Madsen, Chris, 7, 10
Magic City/Magic Empire, xvi, 19, 21,
   24, 26, 46, 75, 90, 91, 134
Main & Easton, 6
Main Street, 2, 4–6, 8, 14, 15, 28,
   37, 39–40, 86, 87, 124
Martin, Linda, 124

Martin, Loyal J., viii, 28, 29,
    37, 40, 42, 70, 77
Maxwell, James L., viii, 104, 106–108, 123
Mayo Building, 67
McAlester, Oklahoma, 7
McAllister, Doug, 119
McClure, H.O., 28
McCormick, Donald, 104
McCullough, Grant, 50, 75
McCune, John W., 94
McCune, Murray, 88, 101, 104
McCune-Jones-McCune, 101
McIntosh, W.E. "Dode," 122
McNulty, Martin J., Jr., 70
Medical Arts Building, 118
Medina, Mike, 126
Meserve, John B., 57
Mid-Century Modern, 88
Mid-Continent Tower, 116, 125
Midland Valley Line, 21
Miscavige, David, 127
Mission School, 56
Missouri-Kansas-Texas
    (the Katy) railroad, 21
Mitchell, John O., viii, 37, 39
Modernism, 102
Mohawk Park, 64, 91
Morning Tulsa Daily World, 41, 43,
    44, 45, 54, 57, 66, 69, 71, 91
Mowbray, Annie (Archer), 9, 10, 12, 14, 20
Mowbray, George W., viii, 8–12, 14,
    15, 18–21, 26, 27, 75, 128
Mowbray, George W., Jr., 14
Mowbray, Grace, 9
Mowbray, Hannah Elizabeth,
    8–10, 12, 14, 20
Mowbray, Helen, 14
Mowbray, Madeline, 14
Mowbray, Mame, 14
Mowbray, Matie (Thomas), 8–10, 14

Municipal Building (1919–1969).
    See also Old City Hall
    blueprint, 61–63
    bonds/funding, 44
    City Commission form
        of government, 33
    condition after vacancy, 111–114
    construction, 57, 65, 67, 70, 71, 134
    design, 60
    Gallery of Mayors, 93
    generally, 41, 59, 64, 91
    during Greenwood fire, 77
    historical preservation, 133
    limitations, 110–111
    memories, 98, 110, 112,
        123, 124, 125, 126
    mural, 71–74, 75, 123
    office space, 107, 116, 120–121, 134
    outgrowing of, 78, 88, 101
    photograph, 68, 85, 92, 96, 108
    sale of, 115, 118, 124, 125, 127, 128
    transfer from Reeder Building, 104
    Urban Renewal and, 109, 110
Municipal Parade & Open House, 96, 97
Murphy, Tom, 126
Muskogee, Oklahoma, 7, 15, 18–19

N

The Nation magazine, 29
National Register of Historic
    Places, 104, 135, 136
Nearly Forgotten (Hicks), 22
Nelson, Dollie, 75
Nelson, Flowers, 16
New York City, 24
Newblock, Herman F., viii, 31,
    42, 75, 77, 78, 85, 91
Nichols, Jerry R., 118, 124–127, 128
Nichols, Wolfe, Stamper, Nally
    & Fallis, 99, 124
Norman, Charles, 107
Norvell, George E., viii, 126

O

Office space, 107, 116, 120–121, 134
Oil Capital of the World, 90
Oil industry, 18–19, 21, 22, 24,
    25, 27, 36, 40, 75, 91
Oklahoma Commissioner of Charities
    and Corrections, 45, 54
Oklahoma statehood, 26
Oklahoma Territory, 10, 26
Old City Hall, xvi, 99, 112, 113, 118, 120,
    122–136.
    See also Municipal Building
    (1919–1969)
Old Mission School, 56
One Technology Center (2007-),
    43, 133–136
Orson, David, 94
Orson, Helen, 94
Orson, Nancy, 94

P

Page, Charles, 75
Page Warehouse, 64
Palace Building, 67, 69
Parking garage/lot, 67, 98, 101, 109
Patterson, Sid, 94, 115, 119
Patton, Daniel Webster,
    viii, 82, 84, 85, 89, 90
Patton, J. Gus, 82, 84
Penney, T.A., viii
Performing Arts Center, 65 n.7, 67
Perry, Oklahoma, 10, 11
Perry Daily Times, 10
Perryman, Andrew, 2, 4–6
Perryman, George, 3, 6
Perryman, Legus, 6
Perryman, Rachel, 6
Perryman and Reed store, 56
Peters, Charles B., xvii
Philtower, 118
Pilkington, J.D., 122, 123
Pioneer District, 56
Pioneer Telephone Company Building, 67

Planning Commission, 85–86, 100
Poe, Lewis M., viii, 15, 16
Police Department, 31, 95
Politics, 16, 18, 26, 31, 70.
    See also Elections
Population growth, 7, 25, 53, 54, 101
Post office, 32, 33
Poteau, Oklahoma, 84
Presbyterian Mission, 55
Presbyterian school, 20
Presbyterians, 18
Price, Lee, Jr., viii, 93
Price, Prior, 15
Public Service Building, 115, 124
Public Service Company of Oklahoma, 124
Public Service Corporation, 44
Purdie, Jack, 99

Q

Quinn, Thomas J., 44, 50, 57

R

Race Riot of 1921, 27, 29, 42, 76, 77
Railroads
    Frisco Depot, 16, 21
    Frisco Railroad, 4, 5, 15, 19, 50
    Midland Valley Line, 21
    Missouri-Kansas-Texas (the
        Katy) railroad, 21
    Santa Fe, 21
    Tulsa's future and, 21
    Union Depot, 86
Randle, Rodger A., viii
Reading & Bates, 125
Red Fork, Oklahoma, 18, 19, 23
Red-light district, 28, 51, 56
Reeder, C.L., viii, 40
Reeder Building (1912-1919), 37, 40, 41,
    43, 45–47, 50, 54, 66, 104, 132–135
Resources Sciences Corporation, 120, 123
Restaurant integration, 107
Retail Merchants' Association, 60
Richardson, Henry Hobson, 64

Rinkovsky, Denise, 38, 39
Roaring Twenties, 89–90, 116, 134
Rogers, Will, 24, 25
Rohde, W. E., viii, 26, 39, 75
Roosevelt, President, 25
Ross Group, 78
Rush, A. William, 60, 64
Rush, E. Arthur, 60, 64
Rush, Endacott & Rush,
    60, 63–66, 71, 78, 113

S
Sand Springs, Oklahoma, 75
Santa Fe, 21
Sapulpa, Oklahoma, 8, 19
Savage, Susan, viii
Schools, 14, 20, 26, 55, 56, 57, 66, 75.
    See also Central High School;
    Tulsa Public Schools
Seaman, J.D., 15
Seaman, J.D. (Mrs. Frank Seaman), 75, 94
2nd & Boston, 37, 40, 41, 47
2nd & Boulder, 38
2nd & Cincinnati, 43
2nd & Main, 31, 38
2nd Street, 33, 39, 43, 44, 87
Senter, Leon, 63
Sewer Department, 101
Sheer, Brad, 99
Shell Creek, 75
Short, E.D., 75
Shutts Building (1910-1912), 37, 40
Simmons, John H., viii, 31, 31 n.16,
    33, 36, 38, 52–55, 57, 58, 60,
    65–67, 70, 71, 104, 128
Simmons Building, 53, 65
Sinclair, Harry, 54
Singer Midgets, 85
Sixth Street, 11
6th & Boulder, 33, 55, 101
6th & Cincinnati, 101, 124
Sky Terrace Room, 78
Snyder Family, 136, 137

Spanish Influenza, 70
Sparks, Jay, 113
Sparks Design, 113
Spavinaw Water Project, 50, 75, 77, 78, 94
Spears, I.H., 76
Springer, William R., 15
Springfield, Missouri, 25
Starr, Belle, 7
State Capitol, 48
Steene, Eula Mae, 73
Steene, William R., 71, 73
Steiner, O.A., 75
Stoner, George H., viii
Stufflebeam, Tom, 15
Sullivan, Louis, 64

T
Tahlequah, Oklahoma, 73
Taylor, Kathy, viii, 134
"The Panorama of Petroleum," 123
3rd & Boulder, 55
3rd & Cheyenne, 33
3rd & Main, 31
3rd Street, 65, 86, 87, 89, 98
Thomas, Beth, 14
Thomas, Harley, 14
Thomas, Henry "Heck," 7–11, 14
Thomas, Matie Mowbray, 8–10, 14
Three Guardsmen, 7, 8
320 South Boston Building, 67, 90
Tilghman, William "Bill," 7, 10, 11
Tollett, Elijah G., Jr., 15, 16
Tracy Park tennis courts, 91
Trail of Tears, 38
Triangle Building, 67
Troy, Frosty, 93
Tulsa, Her Past and Future, 71–74
Tulsa Area United Way, 109
*Tulsa! Biography of the American
    City* (Goble), 107
Tulsa Boosters, 17, 19, 21, 24–26
Tulsa Building, 64
Tulsa City-County Library, 101

Tulsa Club Building, 78, 79, 82
Tulsa Community Chest, 109
Tulsa County Chief, 50
Tulsa County Courthouse, 32, 33, 78, 88
Tulsa Daily World, 28, 38
Tulsa Democrat, 75
Tulsa Federal Building & Post Office, 32, 33
Tulsa Historical Society, 93, 94
Tulsa Plan, 86, 87, 89
Tulsa Public Schools, 4, 26 n.5, 55–56, 78
Tulsa Real Estate Exchange, 78
Tulsa Rose Garden, 91
Tulsa Spirit, 19
Tulsa Tribune, 75, 93, 100, 110, 118
Tulsa World, 38, 98, 124
Tulsa's Magic Roots (Dunn), 18
Turner Store, 13
Twin Territories, 10

U
Union Depot, 86
United States Commissioners Court, 16
United States Congress, 7, 12, 14, 24–25
University of Tulsa, 4, 27
Urban Renewal, xvi, 108–110,
    113, 114, 118, 135
U.S.S. Los Angeles, 90
Utility building, 69

V
Van Witt Fine Art Conservation, 74
Van Witt, Peggy, 74
Vandever Department Store, 37, 40
Vaughn, Clayton, 107, 113
Veale, Clarence H., viii, 92
Vice and crime, 10, 27–28, 30, 31,
    33, 48–49, 51, 56, 75
Vice Trust, 37, 48–50, 53
Voting, 44

W
War Bond Building, 68
War Savings Bank, 68

Warren, Clancy M., viii
Washington, D.C., 24
Water Department, 101
Water supply, 26, 26 n.5, 33,
    50, 75, 77, 78, 94
Watkins, George L., viii, 90
White, Walter F., 75
Whiteside, J.M., 71
Wild Bunch, 10
Williams Auction Company, 74
Williams, Robert L., 48, 49
Williams Brothers, 120
Williams Brothers Engineering
    Company, 123
Williams Brothers Process
    Services, Inc., 123
Williams Center, 13, 65, 67, 86, 87
Williams Communications, 134
Williams, OawEtta, 74
Williams, W.D. "Bill," 74
Winterringer, Gertrude, 14
Winterringer, Grace, 14
Winterringer, Melton, 14
Winterringer, Mildred, 14
Wolfe, Frank B. "Skip," III,
    118, 123–127, 128
Wooden, Frank M., viii, 28, 30, 31, 37,
    40–44, 46–48, 50, 52, 54–57, 65, 70
Woolley, James, 50
Works Progress Administration (WPA), 91
World Association of Detectives, 50
World War I, 54, 93
World War II, 84, 88, 100, 102, 104

Y
YMCA, 33, 67, 69, 98, 99
Young, Terry, viii
Younger, 7
Younkman, C.S., 75

Z
Zeppelin, 90

BIBLIOGRAPHY

Butler, William. *Tulsa 75: A History of Tulsa*. Tulsa, OK: Metropolitan Tulsa Chamber of Commerce, 1974.

Clark, Blue. *Indian Tribes of Oklahoma: A Guide*. Norman: University of Oklahoma Press, 2012.

Cornelius, Jerry L. *Historic Photos of Tulsa*. Nashville, TN: Turner Publishing Company, 2007.

Debo, Angie. *Tulsa: from Creek Town to Oil Capital* Norman: University of Oklahoma Press, 1943.

Douglas, Clarence B. (Col.), *The History of Tulsa, Oklahoma, Vol. I*. Chicago-Tulsa: The S.J. Clarke Publishing Company, 1921.

Douglas, Clarence B. (Col.), *The History of Tulsa, Oklahoma, Vol. II*. Chicago-Tulsa: The S.J. Clarke Publishing Company, 1921.

Douglas, Clarence B. (Col.), *The History of Tulsa, Oklahoma, Vol. III*. Chicago-Tulsa: The S.J. Clarke Publishing Company, 1921.

Dunn, Nina Lane. *Tulsa's Magic Roots*. Tulsa: Oklahoma Book Publishing Company, 1979.

Everly-Douze, Susan. *Tulsa Times: A Pictorial History: Coming of Age*. Tulsa, OK: World Publishing Company, 1988.

Everly-Douze, Susan. *Tulsa Times: A Pictorial History: The Boom Years*. Tulsa, OK: World Publishing Company, 1987.

Everly-Douze, Susan. *Tulsa Times: A Pictorial History: The Early Years*. Tulsa, OK: World Publishing Company, 1986.

Franklin, John Hope, and John Whittington Franklin (ed). *My Life and an Era: The Autobiography of Buck Colbert Franklin*. Baton Rouge and London: Louisiana State University Press, 1997.

Franks, Clyda R., and Kenny Franks. *Images of Tulsa: Where The Streets Were Paved With Gold*. Charleston, SC, Chicago, IL, Portsmouth, NH, San Francisco, CA: Arcadia Publishing, 2000.

Goble, Danney. *Tulsa!: Biography of the American City*. Tulsa, OK: Council Oak Books, 1997.

Hall, James Monroe. *The Beginning of Tulsa*. Tulsa, OK: Tulsa Tribune, 1928.

Hicks, Doug. *Nearly Forgotten: The Amazing Story of the Glenn Pool, Oklahoma's First World-class Oil Field*. Oklahoma: Schnake Turnbo Frank, Inc., 2005.

Hirsch, James S. *Riot and Remembrance: The Tulsa Race War and Its Legacy*. Boston and New York: Houghton Mifflin Company, 2002.

Johnson, Hannibal B. *Black Wall Street: From Riot to Renaissance in Tulsa's Historic Greenwood District*. Fort Worth, Texas: Eakin Press, 1998.

Kemm, James O. *Tulsa: Oil Capital of the World*. Charleston, SC, Chicago, IL, Portsmouth, NH, San Francisco, CA: Arcadia Publishing, 2004.

Lemons, Wishard. *The First Hundred*. Tulsa, OK: First United Methodist Church, 1987.

Shirley, Glenn. *Heck Thomas Frontier Marshal: The Story of a Real Gunfighter*. Philadelphia and New York: Clinton Company, Book Division, 1962.

Thoburn, Joseph B. *A Standard History of Oklahoma: An Authentic Narrative of Its Development from the Date of the First European Exploration Down to the Present Time, Including Accounts of the Indian Tribes, Both Civilized and Wild, of the Cattle Range, of the Land Openings and the Achievements of the Most Recent Period*. Chicago, New York: The American Historical Society, 1916.

Vaughn-Roberson, Courtney Ann, and Glen Vaughn-Roberson. *City in the Osage Hills, Tulsa, Oklahoma*. Boulder, CO: Pruett Publishing Company, 1984.

ABOUT THE AUTHORS

DOUGLAS MILLER is the principal at Müllerhaus Legacy, a Tulsa-based publisher specializing in commissioned history books. Better known for his work as a book designer and publisher, *Seat of Power* is his second effort as lead author following *4th & Boston: Heart of the Magic Empire*. Douglas lives in his beloved Tulsa with his wife, Cher, and their two boys, Jack and James.

JOHN HAMILL first visited Tulsa's Municipal Building as an intern with the *Tulsa Tribune*. Over the years he has written numerous articles about Tulsa for various "annual report" publications/magazines, and was editor of *Tulsa People* magazine during the 1990s. He has authored or contributed to five books on the history of Tulsa. This is his sixth.